Personnel Testing in the Public Safety Industry

A Handbook for Developing and Validating Balanced and Defensible Assessments

Daniel A. Biddle, PhD
Stacy L. Bell-Pilchard, MS

Reference: Biddle, D.A., and Bell-Pilchard, S.L. (2013). Personnel Testing in the Public Safety Industry: A Handbook for Developing and Validating Balanced and Defensible Assessments. Scottsdale, AZ: Infinity Publishing.

Fire & Police Selection, Inc. (FPSI)
193 Blue Ravine Road, Suite 270
Folsom, CA 95630
Office: 1.888.990.3473 | Fax: 916.294.4240
Email: info@FPSI.com
www.FPSI.com | www.NationalFireSelect.com

Editors: Leigh Bashor, PHR; Cheree Ramon

ISBN 978-0-7414-9686-7

Printed in the United States of America

Published July 2013

INFINITY PUBLISHING
1094 New DeHaven Street, Suite 100
West Conshohocken, PA 19428-2713
Toll-free (877) BUY BOOK
Local Phone (610) 941-9999
Fax (610) 941-9959
Info@buybooksontheweb.com
www.buybooksontheweb.com

Contents

Preface iii

Chapter 1—Employment Testing 1
    Title VII of the 1991 Civil Rights Act (CRA) 1
    Adverse Impact: The Trigger for Title VII Litigation 4
    Significance Tests 5

Chapter 2—What Is Validation? 9
    Federal Uniform Guidelines Requirements for Validation 9
    Professional Standards for Validation 9
    Blending the Federal and Professional Standards for Validation 11
    When Tests Exhibit Adverse Impact 12
    Content Validity 13
    Criterion-Related Validity 14
    Benefits of the Validation Process 15

Chapter 3—Written Tests 17
    Steps for Developing Hiring Assessments Using Content Validity 17
    Steps for Developing a Personality Test Using Criterion-Related Validity 25

Chapter 4—Structured Interviews 33
    Developing, Validating, and Analyzing Structured Interviews 33
    Methods for Improving the Interview Process 33
    Types of Questions to Include in Structured Interviews: Situational, Behavioral, and Competency-Based 34
    Steps for Developing Situational Questions 37
    Administering and Scoring an Interview 40

Chapter 5—Developing Valid Work-Sample Physical Ability Tests (PATs).... 43
    Steps for Developing a PAT Using Content Validity 44
    Steps for Developing a PAT Using Criterion-Related Validity 46
    Selecting a Cutoff Time for an Applicant or Incumbent Work-Sample PAT 47
    Administering a PAT 55
    Scoring PATs 58
    The Americans with Disability Act (ADA) and PATs 59
    Sample Test Event Description: Ladder Removal/Carry 60
    Using PATs for Incumbents within Fire Safety 62
    Age and Gender Norming within the Public Safety Industry 67

Chapter 6—Building a Balanced Hiring Program 69
   Challenges and Recommendations for Success 71
   Developing, Validating, and Analyzing Written Tests 75
   Item-Level Analyses 83
   Test-Level Analyses 89
   Weighting Selection Procedures into Combined Scores 106
   Standardizing Scores 109

Chapter 7—Would Your Agency Survive a Legal Challenge? 111
   Content Validation Checklist for Written Tests 111
   Criterion-Related Validation Checklist for Written Tests 112
   Validation Checklist for Structured Interviews 113
   Validation Checklist for Work-Sample Tests or PATs 114
   Validation Checklist for Using Test Results 115

Chapter 8—Lessons from the *Ricci* Case 117
   The *Ricci* Case: An Overview 117
   The Relevance of *Ricci* in the Public Sector 119
   The Strong-Basis-in-Evidence Standard 120
   Applying the *Ricci* Standard to Common Testing Situations 126

Endnotes 131

References 139

Index 143

Preface

This book highlights the key tactics that a strategically-managed public safety department should practice to reduce the likelihood of Equal Employment Opportunity (EEO) lawsuits by diversifying its workforce and making its selection procedures as balanced and defensible as possible. While many of the examples cited in this book are from the fire service industry, they apply equally to law enforcement agencies.

Employers can only avoid or reduce EEO litigation by becoming aware of the basics behind EEO laws and regulations as well as understanding how they work. This includes knowing how litigation is set into motion and how to avoid that. Properly developing and using a balanced set of hiring assessments will help to ensure a diverse, qualified, and well-rounded group of employees.

This book is divided into the following helpful sections for accomplishing this goal:

- Chapter 1 summarizes the basic points of civil rights: Title VII of the 1991 Civil Rights Act, adverse impact (the trigger for Title VII Litigation), and significance.

- Chapter 2 examines the process of validation in more detail and the benefits of developing a valid and effective hiring program.

- Chapter 3 explains the process and benefits of creating written tests using content and criterion-related validity.

- Chapter 4 discusses the importance of using structured interviews and how to develop, validate, and analyze them.

- Chapter 5 describes the steps for developing and validating Physical Ability Tests (PATs) using different validity strategies. This chapter also explains ways to set cutoff scores, the importance of testing both candidates and incumbents, and age and gender norms.

- Chapter 6 identifies the key competencies that should be measured in firefighter and police officer recruitments. This chapter also includes a discussion of written tests, item and test-level analyses, point biserials, Differential Item Functioning, descriptive statistics, psychometric analyses, and the application of cutoff scores.

- Chapter 7 provides useful checklists to ensure that an agency's selection process would withstand court scrutiny.

- Chapter 8 provides an overview of a recent case pertaining to public safety testing and the fine lines between testing, diversity, adverse impact, and equal protection.

Chapter 1—Employment Testing

Title VII of the 1991 Civil Rights Act (CRA)

The Civil Rights Act of 1964 made it illegal for employers to segregate their workforces based on race, or to otherwise consider race when making employment-related decisions. While the vast majority of employers readily adopted and welcomed this much-needed civil rights legislation, some employers continued to conduct illegal selection practices.

On the date that the Civil Rights Act became effective (July 2, 1965), the Duke Power Company established a new policy requiring job applicants for traditionally white classifications (including transfers from other departments) not only to possess a high school diploma, but also to score highly on two separate aptitude tests. Therefore, this policy instituted three potential hurdles to future career advancement.

In 1971, after years of deliberation regarding the validity of these tests relative to the requirements of the at-issue positions, the US Supreme Court ruled in *Griggs v. Duke Power*, by a vote of eight to zero, that the tests constituted an illegal barricade to employment because they did not bear a sufficient connection to the at-issue positions. In essence, the Court ruled that practices that do not assess valid requirements and which cause an "adverse effect" upon a group protected by the Civil Rights Act are illegal.

About one year after this decision, federal civil rights enforcement agencies (the US Equal Employment Opportunity Commission [EEOC] and the Department of Labor's enforcement arm, the Office of Federal Contract Compliance Programs [OFCCP]) began crafting versions of the federal Uniform Guidelines, which were designed to interpret the concepts laid down in the *Griggs* case. In 1978, four federal agencies solidified a set of guidelines that served to interpret the "job relatedness" and "validity" requirements from the *Griggs* case, as reported by the questions and answers section accompanying the Guidelines:

> Question: What is the basic principle of the Guidelines?
>
> Answer: A selection process which has an adverse impact on the employment opportunities of members of a race, color, religion, sex, or national origin group and thus disproportionately screens them out is unlawfully discriminatory unless the process or its component procedures have been validated in accord with the Guidelines, or the user otherwise justifies them in accord with Federal law.... This principle was adopted by the Supreme Court unanimously in *Griggs v.*

Duke Power Co., 401 US 424, and was ratified and endorsed by the Congress when it passed the Equal Employment Opportunity Act of 1972, which amended Title VII of the Civil Rights Act of 1964 (EEOC, 1978).

However, the principles laid down in *Griggs* have not gone without challenge. In 1989, the US Supreme Court handed down a decision that drastically changed the *Griggs* principles that had been incorporated into the Uniform Guidelines. This landmark case, *Ward's Cove Packing Co. v. Atonio* (1989), revised the legal burdens surrounding proof of discrimination from the *Griggs*-based employer's burden (where the employer had to prove that any disparate impact[1] caused by their testing practices was justified by job relatedness/validity), to the burden of proof remaining with the plaintiff at all times. Under *Ward's Cove*, all the employer was required to do was "produce a business justification" that would rationalize the disparate impact — a legal burden much easier to address than the "job-relatedness/business necessity" standard implemented in *Griggs*.

Ward's Cove lasted only two years before being reversed by the 1991 Civil Rights Act (CRA). This act of Congress shifted the validation burden back to the *Griggs* standard by specifically stating the two conditions under which an employer's testing practices would be deemed illegal:

> A(i) a complaining party demonstrates that a respondent uses a particular employment practice that causes a disparate impact on the basis of race, color, religion, sex, or national origin, and the respondent fails to demonstrate that the challenged practice is job-related for the position in question and consistent with business necessity; OR, A(ii) the complaining party makes the demonstration described in subparagraph (C) with respect to an alternate employment practice, and the respondent refuses to adopt such an alternative employment practice. (Section 2000e-2[k][1][A][i])[2]

The above section from the 1991 CRA effectively summarizes the current law of the land with respect to disparate impact and test validation. Notice that the language is job-specific: "the challenged practice is job-related for the position in question and consistent with business necessity." Thus, by definition, evaluating the validity of a test is a test-by-test, job-by-job determination. Also note that Section A(ii) is preceded by the word "OR," indicating that there are two routes available for proving adverse impact; the first is the classic method (adverse impact with no validity), and the second is the demonstration of an "alternative employment practice" that could be used with less adverse impact. While cases have been tried using this latter alternative strategy, this book will focus on the former, the more common classic method.

Since the passage of the 1991 CRA, there has been a steady stream of disparate impact cases in the public safety industry. As of the time of this writing, no cases have changed the foundational framework of the *Griggs* standard as codified in the 1991 CRA.

However, there have been some changes on the legal front regarding the extent to which race-conscious actions can be taken after a testing process has been administered. These changes were spurred by the 2009 US Supreme Court case *Ricci v. DeStefano*, which arose from a lawsuit brought against the City of New Haven, Connecticut, by nineteen City firefighters who claimed that the City discriminated against them with regard to promotions. The firefighters (seventeen whites and two Hispanics) had all passed promotional tests for the captain or lieutenant positions, but because none of the black firefighters scored high enough to be considered for either position, the City invalidated all of the test results. The City claimed that they "feared a lawsuit over the test's disparate impact." (*Ricci*, 2009)

Although there was no real contention about the existence of adverse impact in this case, the City was motivated to prove that the tests were not valid in order to justify its claims that it redacted the exams to uphold the 1991 CRA. The plaintiffs, on the other hand, did not want the validity contested because they wanted the exam results to stand and their scores to be honored. Based on this very unique set of circumstances, a split (five-to-four) decision was rendered by the Court on June 29, 2009. The Court's ruling held that the City's decision to ignore the test results actually violated Title VII of the Civil Rights Act of 1991 and was discriminatory because the City lacked a "strong basis in evidence" that it would have lost a disparate impact lawsuit due to the tests not being sufficiently valid.

Immediately after the case was decided, legal blogs and presentations reacted online, with some even claiming that the *Griggs*/1991 CRA legal foundation had been changed (which was clearly not the case). In response, some courts utilized both the *Ricci* ruling and the *Griggs* ruling in their arguments to emphasize that the 1991 CRA standard was still very much upheld. One such case was *Vulcan Society v. City of New York* (2009) which was decided just weeks after the *Ricci* ruling. In *Vulcan*, the judge clarified the distinctions between the *Ricci* ruling (which focused on specific disparate treatment in regard to a test) and typical disparate impact cases:

> Before proceeding to the legal analysis, (we) offer a brief word about the Supreme Court's recent decision in *Ricci*.... (we) reference *Ricci* not because the Supreme Court's ruling controls the outcome in this case; to the contrary, (we) mention *Ricci* precisely to point out that it does not. In *Ricci*, the City of New Haven had set aside the results of a promotional examination, and the Supreme Court confronted the narrow issue of whether New Haven could defend a violation of Title

VII's disparate treatment provision by asserting that its challenged employment action was an attempt to comply with Title VII's disparate impact provision. The Court held that such a defense is only available when 'the employer can demonstrate a strong basis in evidence that, had it not taken the action, it would have been liable under the disparate impact statute' (Id. at 2664). In contrast, this case presents the entirely separate question of whether Plaintiffs have shown that the City's use of [the Exams] has actually had a disparate impact upon black and Hispanic applicants for positions as entry-level firefighters. *Ricci* did not confront that issue.... The relevant teaching of *Ricci*, in this regard, is that the process of designing employment examinations is complex, requiring consultation with experts and careful consideration of accepted testing standards. As discussed below, these requirements are reflected in federal regulations and existing Second Circuit precedent. This legal authority sets forth a simple principle: municipalities must take adequate measures to ensure that their civil service examinations reliably test the relevant knowledge, skills and abilities that will determine which applicants will best perform their specific public duties. (Biddle and Bell-Pilchard, 2012)

The gears of several disparate impact cases continued to turn during and after the *Ricci* case, with the *Griggs* standard in full effect. Should a case come along some day that does change the *Griggs* standard, a commensurate change to the Uniform Guidelines will also likely be required. See Chapter 8 for further discussion of the *Ricci* case.

Adverse Impact: The Trigger for Title VII Litigation

Each situation where a Title VII claim is made has a common denominator: adverse impact. The way the federal law currently stands, plaintiffs cannot bring a lawsuit unless and until a test causes adverse impact. Because this trigger underlies all EEO-related litigation (at least of the disparate impact variety), it is imperative to clearly define and understand adverse impact.

Rather than enter into a lengthy academic definition of adverse impact, the topic will be simplified into a few, concise paragraphs.[3] When discussing adverse impact, the most relevant terms for the purposes of this book have to do with significance: the 80% test, statistical significance, and practical significance.

Significance Tests

80% Test

This test is used to determine the presence of adverse impact and is calculated by dividing the focal group's (typically minorities or women) passing rate on a test by the reference group's (typically whites or men) passing rate. Any value resulting in less than 80% constitutes a violation of this test. This test was originally framed in 1972, was codified in the Uniform Guidelines in 1978, and has been referenced in hundreds of court cases (Biddle, 2011). However, despite its widespread use, it should not be regarded as the final litmus test for uncovering adverse impact. That position is held exclusively by statistical significance tests, which are described next.

Statistical Significance

A "statistically significant" finding is one that gives the researcher reasonable cause to think that something has been detected that is not likely the result of chance. If a researcher conducts an adverse impact analysis and obtains a statistically significant result, he or she can state (with a reasonable level of certainty) that a legitimate trend, and not a chance relationship, actually exists.

Statistical significance tests result in a p-value (p for probability), with p-values ranging from 0 to +1. A p-value of 0.01 means that the odds of the event occurring by chance are only 1%. A p-value of 1.0 means that there is essentially a 100% certainty that the event is merely a chance occurrence and cannot be considered as a meaningful finding. A p-value of .05 or less is said to be statistically significant in the realm of EEO analyses. This .05 level (or 5%) corresponds with the odds ratio of one chance in twenty. This 5% chance level is the p-value threshold that has been endorsed in nearly every adverse impact case or federal enforcement setting.

Conducting a statistically significant adverse impact analysis is very straightforward, provided that a statistical software program is used.[4] The process is completed by applying a statistical test to a 2 X 2 table, where the success rates of two groups are compared. See the following example.

2 X 2 Table Example

Group	Promoted	Not Promoted
Whites	30	20
Asians	20	30

There are over twenty possible statistical tests that can be used for computing the statistical significance of a 2 X 2 table, including estimation and exact methods, and there are various models that make certain assumptions regarding how the 2 X 2 table

5

itself is constructed (Biddle and Morris, 2011). For example, using an estimation technique (such as the Chi-Square computation) on the table above returns a p-value of .046 (below the .05 level needed for a statistically significant finding); whereas, using a more precise method (the Fisher's Exact Test with Lancaster's mid-P Correction)[5] returns a p-value of .06 (not significant).

Practical Significance

The concept of practical significance in the EEO analysis field was first introduced in Section 4D of the Uniform Guidelines ("Smaller differences in selection rate may nevertheless constitute adverse impact, where they are significant in both statistical and practical terms…"). Practical significance tests are applied to adverse impact analyses to evaluate the "practical impact" (typically reported as the shortfall pertaining to the group with the lower passing rate) or "stability" of the results (evaluating whether a statistically significant finding still exists after changing the passing/failing numbers of the disadvantaged group). While this concept enjoyed a run in the federal court system (Biddle, 2011), it has more recently been met with a considerable level of disagreement and condemnation in the courts.[6] For example, in the most recent circuit level case dealing with practical significance, the court stated:

> Similarly, this Court has never established 'practical significance' as an independent requirement for a plaintiff's prima facie disparate impact case, and we decline to do so here. The EEOC Guidelines themselves do not set out 'practical significance' as an independent requirement, and we find that in a case in which the statistical significance of some set of results is clear, there is no need to probe for additional 'practical' significance. Statistical significance is relevant because it allows a fact-finder to be confident that the relationship between some rule or policy and some set of disparate impact results was not the product of chance. This goes to the plaintiff's burden of introducing statistical evidence that is 'sufficiently substantial' to raise 'an inference of causation.' *Watson*, 487 US at 994-95. There is no additional requirement that the disparate impact caused be above some threshold level of practical significance. Accordingly, the District Court erred in ruling 'in the alternative' that the absence of practical significance was fatal to Plaintiffs' case. (*Stagi v. National Railroad Passenger Corporation*, 2010; and Biddle and Bell-Pilchard, 2012)

For these reasons, while the Uniform Guidelines are clear that practical significance evaluations (such as shortfalls and statistical significance stability tests) are conceptually relevant to adverse impact analyses, employers should use caution when evaluating the practical significance of adverse impact analysis results. While the concept is relevant, it will ultimately be left for a judge to decide whether (and to what extent) practical significance can be used in court. Certainly, it would be a risky endeavor to adopt hard-and-fast practical significance rules when analyzing adverse impact.

Chapter 2—What Is Validation?

Federal Uniform Guidelines Requirements for Validation

The current government treatise for validation is the 1978 federal Uniform Guidelines. These guidelines were assembled in a mutual effort by the EEOC, the Civil Service Commission, the Department of Labor, and the Department of Justice. The goal of publishing the Uniform Guidelines was to provide an objective standard by which testing and adverse impact concepts could be defined and used for government enforcement, arbitration, and litigation. Numerous earlier texts and enforcement guidelines existed prior to the Uniform Guidelines, but it is safe to say that the Uniform Guidelines constituted the most definitive treatise at the time of its publication. The Uniform Guidelines remain mostly unchanged.

Three primary forms of validation are presented in the Uniform Guidelines—content, criterion-related, and construct-related. The list below is in the order most frequently used by employers:

- Content validity. Demonstrated by data showing that the content of a selection procedure is representative of important aspects of on-the-job performance (Sections 5B and 14C).

- Criterion-related validity. Demonstrated by empirical data showing that the selection procedure is predictive of or significantly correlated with important elements of work behavior (Sections 5B and 14B).

- Construct validity. Demonstrated by data showing that the selection procedure measures the degree to which candidates have identifiable characteristics that have been determined to be important for successful job performance (Sections 5B and 14D).

Professional Standards for Validation

In the early 1950s, the three different aspects of validity (content, criterion-related, and construct) were discussed. From the 1950s through the publication of the 1978 Uniform Guidelines, these were the most commonly used validation strategies (especially in litigation settings). While the Uniform Guidelines set these validation ground rules in 1978, the government anticipated that the educational and personnel testing fields would continue to advance the science and art of validation. It, therefore, included the following provision for considering future developments in framing the criteria that will be used for validating selection procedures:

For the purposes of satisfying these guidelines, users may rely upon criterion-related validity studies, content validity studies or construct validity studies, in accordance with the standards set forth in the technical standards of these guidelines, Section 14 of this part. New strategies for showing the validity of selection procedures will be evaluated as they become accepted by the psychological profession. (Section 5A)

Fulfilling this expectation, the psychological community authored two documents. One was the 1985 version of the Standards for Educational and Psychological Testing, also known as the Standards, which was published by the American Educational Research Association (AERA), the American Psychological Association (APA), and the National Council on Measurement in Education. The other document was published by Division 14 of the APA, the Society for Industrial and Organizational Psychology (SIOP), Principles for the Validation and Use of Personnel Selection Procedures (also known as the 1987 SIOP Principles).

These two documents advanced the testing field to the current state of validation. Fourteen years later, the Standards were substantially updated (AERA, 1999). Following suit, the SIOP Principles received a major update sixteen years later in 2003. While published by different associations, the Principles and Standards virtually agree on the key aspects of validity. Part of the motivating factor behind the publication of the revised Principles was to provide an update to the earlier version based on the newly published Standards.

At the heart of these two documents is how they define validity. Both the Standards and the Principles have moved from defining validity in terms of the three conventional types of validity (like those discussed in the Uniform Guidelines), toward a definition of "validity as a unitary concept with different sources of evidence contributing to an understanding of the inferences that can be drawn from a selection procedure" (SIOP, 2003).

The Standards and Principles allow five different sources to generate validity evidence under this umbrella; they are the:

1. relationships between predictor scores and other variables, such as selection procedure-criterion relationships;

2. content (meaning the questions, tasks, format, and wording of questions, response formats, and guidelines regarding administration and scoring of the selection procedure. Evidence based on selection procedure content may include logical or empirical analyses that compare the adequacy of the match between selection procedure content and work content, worker requirements, or outcomes of the job);

3. internal structure of the selection procedure (e.g., how well items on a test cluster together);

4. response processes (examples given in the Principles include (a) questioning test takers about their response strategies, (b) analyzing examinee response times on computerized assessments, or (c) conducting experimental studies where the response set is manipulated); and,

5. consequences of testing.

The Principles explain that these five sources are not distinct types of validity, but "each provides information that may be highly relevant to some proposed interpretations of scores, and less relevant, or even irrelevant to others" (2003).

Blending the Federal and Professional Standards for Validation

How are the professional standards different from the government standards? How are they similar? All three types of validation described in the Uniform Guidelines are also contained in the professional standards (SIOP Principles and 1999 Standards):

- The content validity described in the Uniform Guidelines is similar to the "validation evidence," to a limited degree, of the professional standards.

- The criterion-related validity described in the Uniform Guidelines is similar to Standards 1 and 5.

- The construct validity described in the Uniform Guidelines is similar to Standards 1, 3, and 5.

When conducting a validation study, which set of standards should a practitioner be most concerned about—the Principles, the Standards, or the Uniform Guidelines? The conservative answer is all three, but if one had to choose a primary set of criteria, here are a few reasons for choosing the Uniform Guidelines:

- They are endorsed by the US government (the EEOC, OFCCP, Department of Labor, Department of Justice, and nearly every state's fair-employment office).

- They are regularly used as the set of criteria for weighing validity studies during enforcement audits conducted by the OFCCP and numerous other state fair-employment offices.

- They have been consistently used by the courts as the measuring stick for assessing the merit of validity studies.

- They have been referenced thousands of times in judicial documents. By contrast, as of the year 2000, the Principles have only been referenced in thirteen federal court cases and the Standards in ten, the former of which was also cited as "less than instructive." (*Lanning v. Southeastern Pennsylvania Transportation Authority*, 1999)[7]

- They inherently include the key elements of the Standards and Principles, while the reciprocal is only true for some sources of validation evidence espoused by the professional standards.

The Principles and Standards do offer more guidelines and regulations than the Uniform Guidelines, and provide more complete guidance for many unique circumstances that emerge in testing situations. However, for the reasons stated above, the Uniform Guidelines are the primary set of criteria that will be addressed throughout this text as the standard for completing validation studies.

Of the three validation types proposed in the Uniform Guidelines, this book will only focus on content and criterion-related validity. Construct validity will not be discussed further for a few key reasons. First, the authors are not aware of any EEO-related case where a judge has endorsed a validation study based solely on construct validity. The concept is highly academic and theoretical, so it is difficult for even advanced practitioners to build selection procedures based solely on construct validity. With this being the case, expert witnesses will find themselves hard-pressed to explain such concepts to a judge. Second, if one were to ask one hundred validation experts to define construct validity, almost as many unique definitions would emerge, several even contradicting each other. Third, most forms of construct validity require some type of criterion-related validity evidence. All of this simply begs the question: Why not just use content and criterion-related validity in the first place? For these reasons, readers are referred to other texts if they desire to review the concept of construct validity in more depth (Cascio, 1998; and Gatewood, 1994).

When Tests Exhibit Adverse Impact

Test validation is often misunderstood. While validation is a legal obligation whenever an employer's test exhibits adverse impact, it is much more than that. Validation is actually a scientific process for ensuring that your department's testing process focuses on the key competencies that are needed for job success. Hiring without a properly validated process is like pulling names out of a hat. Validation has at least two key benefits: (1) utility (the benefits to employers of hiring highly qualified candidates), and (2) legal defensibility.

Techniques and Legal Requirements for Testing

The two validation strategies that are most frequently applied in practice are content validity and criterion-related validity; both are supported by the Uniform Guidelines, professional standards, and numerous court cases. While there are several possible ways to develop tests under either strategy, the most basic components of each are discussed below.

Content Validity

Content validity evidence is gathered by demonstrating a connection between the test and important job requirements. When conducted from the beginning, a content validation study will include at least the following steps:

1. Conduct a job analysis—establishing strong content validity evidence begins with having a clear understanding of what the job requires, especially the areas that are targeted by the test. Generally speaking, content validity evidence is made stronger by developing and implementing a thorough job analysis process.

2. Develop a clear test plan—a test plan identifies the key Knowledge, Skills, Abilities, and Personal Characteristics (KSAPCs) identified by the job analysis process as being necessary on the first day of employment. Ideally, only the most important KSAPCs are included in the test plan.

3. Connect the test to the job—a process needs to be completed that establishes or demonstrates a clear connection between the test and the important job KSAPCs. This connection can be demonstrated by using the opinions from methodology (testing) and/or job experts. Ultimately, the KSAPCs measured by the test need to be linked to the important KSAPCs of the job, which are then linked to the important job duties. This three-way process establishes content validity.

4. Establish how the tests will be used—adopting a content validity process requires using the test results in a way that accurately reflects how the important KSAPCs measured by the test are actually applied on the job (e.g., ranking, pass/fail, banded—see Chapter 6). For example, possessing basic math skills is necessary to be a competent public safety officer, but possessing increasingly higher levels of this skill does not necessarily translate into superior on-the-job performance. Other abilities, such as teamwork and interpersonal skills, are more likely to differentiate performance between officers when held at above-minimum levels. Following in this same spirit, tests measuring basic math should be used on a pass/fail (cutoff) basis, whereas tests measuring differentiating KSAPCs should be the primary basis for hiring decisions. A complete discussion of test-use considerations is provided in Chapter 6.

Criterion-Related Validity

Criterion-related validity is statistical in nature and is established by demonstrating a significant correlation between the test and some important aspect of job performance. For example, a department might have the supervisory staff assign job performance ratings to the incumbents, run the incumbents through a Physical Ability Test (PAT), and then conduct a statistical analysis between the test and job performance ratings to assess whether they are significantly correlated.

Criterion-related validity studies can be conducted in one of two ways: by using a predictive model or a concurrent model. A predictive model is conducted when applicant test scores are correlated to subsequent measures of job performance (e.g., six months after the tested applicants are hired). A concurrent model is conducted by giving a test to incumbents (employees who are presently on the job) and then correlating their scores to their own measures of current job performance (e.g., performance review scores, supervisor ratings, etc.). The following steps can be completed to conduct a concurrent criterion-related validity study:

1. Be sure that your department has at least one hundred and fifty subjects to include in the study. This minimum sample size is recommended because, in most situations, it provides adequate statistical power for detecting a meaningful correlation (e.g., a sample size of one hundred and thirty-four provides a 90% likelihood of finding a .25 correlation, if such a correlation exists in the target population).

2. Conduct a job analysis to determine the important aspects of the job that should be included in the study (both from the testing side and the rating side).

3. Develop one or more criterion measures of subjective (e.g., job- performance rating scales) or objective measures (e.g., absenteeism and work output levels) of critical areas from the job analysis. A subjectively rated criterion should only consist of performance on a job duty (or group of duties). In most cases, it should not consist of a supervisor/coworker rating the incumbent's level of KSAPCs (a requirement based on Section 15B5 of the Uniform Guidelines) unless the KSAPCs are clearly linked to observable work behaviors, or they are sufficiently operationally defined. It is important that these measures have sufficiently high reliability (at least .60 or higher is preferred).

4. Work with job experts and supervisors, trainers, other management staff, and the job analysis data to form solid speculations (hypotheses) regarding which KSAPCs are the strongest predictors of high or low scores of such job-performance measures (above).

5. Develop tests that reliably measure those KSAPCs. Choosing tests that have reliability of .70 or higher is preferred.[8]

6. Administer the tests and correlate the scores with the criterion measures via a Pearson Correlation analysis. To perform a Pearson Correlation in Microsoft Excel®, use the =PEARSON command and evaluate the results.

The resulting correlation coefficient must, at a minimum, be statistically significant at the .05 level (before making any corrections). Ideally, it should also be sufficiently strong to result in practical implications for the hiring process. The US Department of Labor has provided reasonable guidelines for interpreting correlation coefficients, with coefficients between .21 and .35 classified as "likely to be useful" and coefficients higher than .35 as "very beneficial" (2000).

Benefits of the Validation Process

Now that validation has been briefly defined, what is its value to the employer? Why validate selection procedures? "Validation is expensive," and "We are only required to validate a selection procedure if it has adverse impact" (a true statement) are typical responses that personnel consultants frequently hear. Formal validation studies can cost in the tens of thousands of dollars, making these legitimate concerns.

Regardless of the costs, validation generates at least two major benefits for the employer. First, validation helps ensure that the selection process is measuring key and relevant job requirements in a reliable and consistent manner. This, of course, helps select better workers into the workforce. Even if the validation process only slightly increases the effectiveness of a selection process, the results over years or hundreds of applicants can be astounding. Second, the validation process generates evidence (which can be used in the event of litigation) that the selection procedures are "job related for the position in question and consistent with business necessity" (to address the requirements of the 1991 Civil Rights Act, Section 703[k][1][A][i]).

Related to the latter benefit, validated selection procedures can also dissuade potential plaintiffs from ever beginning the lawsuit process if the relationship between the selection procedure and the job is somewhat self-evident (has "face validity"). Applicants are much less likely to challenge a selection procedure if it resembles the actual job. Likewise, plaintiff attorneys will be discouraged from gambling the time and money necessary to wage an arduous legal battle if the employer has already conducted good-faith validation studies.

Chapter 3—Written Tests

Job knowledge can be defined as "the accumulation of facts, principles, concepts and other pieces of information that are considered important in the performance of one's job" (Dye, Reck, and McDaniel, 1993). As applied to written tests in the personnel setting, knowledge can be categorized as: declarative knowledge—knowledge of technical information, or procedural knowledge—knowledge of the processes and judgmental criteria required to perform correctly and efficiently on the job (Hunter and Hunter, 1984; and Dye et al., 1993).

While job knowledge is not typically critical for many entry-level positions, it clearly has its place in many supervisory positions where having a command of certain knowledge areas is essential for job performance. For example, if a fire captain responsible for instructing firefighters who have been deployed to extinguish a house fire does not possess a mastery-level of knowledge (see Step 1: Conduct a Job Analysis, item 5, below for description) required for the task, the safety of the firefighters and the public could be in jeopardy. This is because it is not feasible for a fire captain to refer to textbooks during an emergency; rather, he or she must already have the particular knowledge memorized.

There are a variety of steps that should be followed to ensure that a job-knowledge written test is developed and utilized properly. Depending upon the size and type of the employer, they may be faced with litigation from state or federal regulatory agencies or a private plaintiff attorney. Each year, employers accused of utilizing tests that have adverse impact spend millions of dollars defending litigated promotional processes.[9]

In litigation settings, addressing these standards is typically conducted by completing a validation study (using any of the acceptable types of validity). This section outlines seven steps for developing a job-related and court-defensible plan for creating a content-valid, job-knowledge written test used for hiring or promoting employees.

Steps for Developing Hiring Assessments Using Content Validity

The steps below are designed to address the essential requirements based on the Uniform Guidelines (1978), the Principles (2003), and the Standards (1999):[10]

Step 1: Conduct a Job Analysis

The foundational requirement for developing a content-valid, job-knowledge written test is a current and thorough job analysis for the target position. Brief, vague, and/or simplified job descriptions are almost never sufficient for showing validity under the Uniform Guidelines unless, at a bare minimum, they include:

- job expert input and/or review;
- job duties and KSAPCs that are essential for the job; and,
- operationally-defined KSAPCs.

In practice, where validity is required, updated job analyses typically need to be developed. Ideally, creating a Uniform Guidelines-style job analysis would include the following ratings for job duties:

(1) Frequency (Uniform Guidelines, Sections 15B3 and 14D4)[11]

This duty is performed (select one option from below) *by me or other active* (target position) *in my department.*

1. annually or less often
2. semiannually (approximately two times/year)
3. quarterly (approximately four times/year)
4. monthly (approximately one time/month)
5. biweekly (approximately every two weeks)
6. weekly (approximately one time/week)
7. semiweekly (approximately two times/week)
8. daily/infrequently (approximately one to six times/day)
9. daily/frequently (approximately seven or more times/day)

(2) Importance (Uniform Guidelines, Sections 14C1, 2, 4; 14D2, 3; 15C3, 4, 5; and 15D3)

Competent performance of this duty is (select one option from below) *for the job of* (target position) *in my department.*

1. not important: of minor significance to the performance of the job.
2. of some importance: somewhat useful and/or meaningful to the performance of the job. Improper performance may result in slight negative consequences.
3. important: useful and/or meaningful to the performance of the job. Improper performance may result in moderate negative consequences.
4. critical: necessary for the performance of the job. Improper performance may result in serious negative consequences.
5. very critical: necessary for the performance of the job and with more extreme consequences. Improper performance may result in very serious negative consequences.

(3) Differentiating Best-Worker Ratings (Uniform Guidelines, Section 14C9)

Possessing above-minimum levels of this KSAPC makes (select one option from below) *difference in overall job performance.*

1. no
2. little
3. some
4. a significant
5. a very significant

Note: Obtaining ratings on the Best-Worker scale is not necessary if the job-knowledge written test will be used only on a pass/fail basis (rather than ranking final test results).

(4) When Needed (Uniform Guidelines, Sections 5F and 14C1)

Possessing (select one option from below) *of this KSAPC is needed upon entry to the job for the* (target position) *position in your department.*

1. none or very little
2. some (less than half)
3. most (more than half)
4. all or almost all

In addition to these four KSAPC rating scales, it is recommended that a mastery-level scale be used when validating written job-knowledge tests. The data from these ratings is useful for choosing the job knowledge that should be included in a written job-knowledge test, to address Section 14C4 of the Uniform Guidelines, which requires that job knowledge measured on a test be operationally defined as "that body of learned information which is used in and is a necessary prerequisite for observable aspects of work behavior of the job." It is recommended to use an average rating threshold of 3.0 on the mastery-level scale for selecting which job knowledge to include on job-knowledge tests. A sample mastery-level scale is listed below:

(5) Mastery Level (Uniform Guidelines, Section 14C4)

A (select one option from below) *level of this job knowledge is necessary for successful job performance.*

1. low: none or only a few general concepts or specifics must be available in memory in no, or only a few, circumstances without referencing materials or asking questions.

2. familiarity: have some general concepts and some specifics available in memory in some circumstances without referencing materials or asking questions.

3. working knowledge: have most general concepts and most specifics available in memory in most circumstances without referencing materials or asking questions.

4. mastery: have almost all general concepts and almost all specifics available in memory in almost all circumstances without referencing materials or asking questions.

Finally, a duty/KSAPC linkage scale should be used to ensure that the KSAPCs are necessary for the performance of important job duties. A sample duty/KSAPC linkage scale is provided below:

(6) Duty/KSAPC Linkages (Uniform Guidelines, Section 14C4)

This KSAPC is (select one option from below) *for the performance of this duty.*

1. not important
2. of minor importance
3. important
4. of major importance
5. critically important

When job experts identify KSAPCs necessary for the job, it is helpful if they are written in a way that maximizes the likelihood of job/duty linkages. When KSAPCs fail to provide enough content to link to job duties, their inclusion in a job analysis is of limited benefit. The following are examples of a poorly-written and a well-written KSAPC from a firefighter job analysis:

- Example of a poorly-written KSAPC: *Knowledge of ventilation practices.*
- Example of a well-written KSAPC: *Knowledge of ventilation practices and techniques to release contained heat, smoke, and gases in order to enter a building. Includes application of appropriate fire suppression techniques and equipment (including manual and power tools and ventilation fans).*

Step 2: Develop a Selection Plan

The first step in developing a selection plan is to review the KSAPCs from the job analysis and design a plan for measuring the essential KSAPCs using various selection procedures (particularly knowledge areas). At a minimum, the knowledge areas selected for the test should be important and necessary on the first day of the job, required at some level of mastery (rather than easily looked up without hindrance on the job), and appropriately measured using a written test format. All job knowledge that meets these criteria is selected for inclusion in the test plan outlined below.

Step 3: Create a Test Plan

Once the KSAPCs that will be measured on the test have been identified, the test sources relevant for the knowledge should be identified. Review relevant job-related materials and discuss the target job in considerable detail with job experts. This will focus attention on job-specific information for the job under analysis. Review the knowledge areas that meet the necessary criteria and determine which sources and/or textbooks are best suited to measure them. It is imperative that the content of the selected sources is not contradictory.

Once the test sources have been identified, determine whether or not preparatory materials will be offered to the applicants. If preparatory materials are used, ensure that the materials are current, specific, and released to all applicants taking the test. In addition to preparatory materials, determine if preparatory sessions will be offered to the applicants.

Use of preparatory sessions appears to be beneficial to both minority and non-minority applicants, although such sessions do not consistently reduce adverse impact (Sackett, Schmitt, Ellingson, and Kabin, 2001). If study sessions are conducted, make every attempt to schedule the sessions at a location that is geographically convenient for all applicants and at a reasonable time of day. Invite all applicants to attend and provide plenty of notice of the dates and times.

Following the identification of the knowledge areas and source materials that will be used to develop the job-knowledge written test, identify the number of items that will be included on the test. Be sure to include enough items to ensure high test reliability. Typically, job-knowledge tests that are made up of similar job-knowledge domains will generate reliability levels in the high .80s to the low .90s when they include eighty items or more.

Consider using job expert input to determine internal weights for the written test. Provide job experts with a list of the different knowledge areas to be measured and ask them to distribute one hundred points among the knowledge areas in order to obtain a balanced written test. See Table 3-1 for a sample of a knowledge-weighting survey used to develop a written test for certifying firefighters (this type of test would be used by fire departments that only hire pre-trained firefighters into entry-level positions).

Table 3-1. Firefighter Development Survey

Firefighter Development Survey	
Job Expert Name: _____ Date: _____	
Instructions: Assume that you have $100 to "buy" the perfect firefighter for your department based only on job-knowledge qualifications. Also assume other important areas such as physical abilities and interpersonal skills have already been accounted for. How much money would you spend, in each of the following job-knowledge areas, to "buy the most qualified firefighter" for your department? Your total allocations should equal exactly $100.	
Knowledge Sources (Fire Service Books)	Dollars You Would Spend to "Buy" the Perfect Firefighter
Pumping Apparatus Driver/Operator Handbook	
Principles of Vehicle Extrication	
Fire Department Company Officer	
Fire and Emergency Services Instructor	
Aerial Apparatus Driver/Operator Handbook	
Essentials of Firefighting	
Rapid Intervention Teams	
The Source Book for Fire Company Training Evolutions	
Fire Inspection and Code Enforcement	
Hazardous Materials	
TOTAL (must equal $100)	

Attempt to obtain an adequate sampling of the knowledge, and ensure that there are a sufficient number of items developed to effectively measure each at the desired level. Note that some knowledge will require more items than others to ensure a more thorough assessment. The test should be internally weighted in a way that ensures a sufficient measurement of the relevant knowledge areas.

Choose the types of items that will be included on the test following the determined length of the test and the number of items to be derived from each source. One helpful tool is a process-by-content matrix to ensure adequate sampling of job-knowledge content areas and problem-solving processes. Problem-solving levels include:

- Definition: knowledge of the terminology related to the job;
- Principle: understanding of the principles employed on the job – where the basic concepts of the areas assessed need to be understood; and,
- Application: application of knowledge to new situations – where an even greater level of mastery is required.

The job-knowledge written test should include test items from all three levels to ensure the applicants can define important terms related to the job as well as be able to apply their knowledge of the principles of the job to answer more complex questions. Job experts should consider how the knowledge is applied and required on the job when determining the types of items to be included on the final test form (see Table 3-2 for a sample process-by-content matrix for a fire captain written test).

Table 3-2. Process-by-Content Matrix: Fire Captain

Process-by-Content Matrix: Fire Captain				
Knowledge Sources (Fire Service Books)	Definition	Principle	Application	Total
1. Brady Emergency Care	4	10	20	34
2. Brunacini, Fire Command	3	7	13	23
3. Fire Chief's Handbook	3	10	17	30
4. IFSTA Building Construction	1	3	6	10
5. IFSTA Wildland Firefighting	4	5	9	18
6. IFSTA Fire Service Rescue	4	6	10	20
7. IFSTA Essentials	2	2	6	10
8. IFSTA Chief Officer	0	1	1	2
9. IFSTA Hazardous Materials	0	1	2	3
Total	21	45	84	150

Step 4: Develop the Test Content

After the number and types of test items to be developed have been determined, select a diverse panel of four to ten job experts (who have a minimum of one year experience each) to review the test plan to ensure that it complies with the parameters. Have each job expert sign a confidentiality agreement. If the job experts will be writing the test items, provide item-writing training and have job experts write, exchange, and review the items.

Once the job experts have written the items to be included in the test bank, ensure proper grammar, style, and consistency. Additionally, make certain that the test plan requirements are met. Once the bank of test items has been created, provide the final test version to the panel of job experts for the validation process .

Step 5: Validate the Test

Validating the test is the most important step in this entire process. The validation process is completed by convening a panel of qualified job experts and having them provide ratings on several factors that are relevant to the test items and the job analysis for the target position. While the questions on the validation survey will vary widely across departments and testing consultants, the basic goal is the same: to establish a job-related connection between the test items and the target job.

Whatever system is used, it is critical to include survey questions that will address the fundamental requirements of the federal Uniform Guidelines and professional testing guidelines (e.g., the Principles and the Standards). Figure 3-1 below provides a survey that is used as part of the Test Validation & Analysis Program

(TVAP™),[12] published by Biddle Consulting Group, Inc., to guide professionals through the process of validating and analyzing written tests. This survey includes the key factors that should be evaluated by job experts during a written test validation process.

Figure 3-1. Test Validation Survey (from the BCG Test Validation & Analysis Program)

Name: _____ Test: _____ Date: _____		Test Item Number		
		#1	#2	#3...
1. Does the item <u>STEM</u>:				
A. READ WELL? (Is it <u>CLEAR</u> and <u>UNDERSTANDABLE</u>?)	N/Y	N Y	N Y	N Y
B. Provide <u>SUFFICIENT INFORMATION</u> to answer correctly?	N/Y	N Y	N Y	N Y
2. Are the <u>DISTRACTORS</u>:				
A. Similar in difficulty?	N/Y	N Y	N Y	N Y
B. Distinct?	N/Y	N Y	N Y	N Y
C. Incorrect, yet plausible?	N/Y	N Y	N Y	N Y
D. Similar in length?	N/Y	N Y	N Y	N Y
E. Correctly matching to the stem?	N/Y	N Y	N Y	N Y
3. Is the key <u>CORRECT IN ALL CIRCUMSTANCES</u>?	N/Y	N Y	N Y	N Y
4. Is this item <u>FREE OF PROVIDING CLUES</u> to other items?	N/Y	N Y	N Y	N Y
5. Is this item <u>FREE FROM UNNECESSARY COMPLEXITIES</u>?	N/Y	N Y	N Y	N Y
6. What percent of <u>MINIMALLY QUALIFIED APPLICANTS</u> would you expect to answer this item correctly?	%			
7. Is this item <u>FAIR</u> to all groups of people?	N/Y	N Y	N Y	N Y
8. What <u>JOB DUTY</u> is represented by this item?	# from Job Analysis			
9. What <u>KSAPC</u> is being measured by this item?				
10. Does the item measure a part of the KSAPC that is <u>NECESSARY ON THE FIRST DAY</u> of the job?	N/Y	N Y	N Y	N Y
Only Answer Items 11-14 Below for Job Knowledge Test Items				
11. Is the item <u>BASED ON CURRENT INFORMATION</u>?	N/Y	N Y	N Y	N Y
12. How important is it that the knowledge tested be <u>MEMORIZED</u>? 0 - NOT NECESSARY: can be looked up without impacting job performance 1 - IMPORTANT: negative job impact is LIKELY if it had to be looked up 2 - ESSENTIAL: negative job impact is MOST LIKELY if it had to be looked up	0-2			
13. Does the <u>LEVEL OF DIFFICULTY</u> of the item correspond to the level of difficulty of the knowledge as used on the job?	N/Y	N Y	N Y	N Y
14. How serious are the <u>CONSEQUENCES</u> if the applicant does not possess the knowledge required to answer this item correctly? 0 - LITTLE or NO consequences 1 - MODERATE consequences 2 - SEVERE consequences	0-2			

After the ratings are collected from job experts for each item on the test using the TVAP survey, the program applies criteria derived from court cases, the federal Uniform Guidelines, and professional testing standards to mark each item as valid or not valid and sets a passing score for the test using the modified Angoff procedure (see below). Whatever system is used, the fundamental questions displayed in Figure 3-1 should be included and addressed by the validation and rating process.

Additionally, have the job experts identify an appropriate time limit for the test. A common rule of thumb is to allow one minute per test item plus thirty additional minutes overall (e.g., a 150-item test would yield a three-hour time limit).[13] A time limit is considered reasonable if it allows for at least 95% of the applicants to complete the test within the allotted time.[14]

Step 6: Compile the Test

Test items that survive the validation review process should be compiled into a final test form and an unmodified Angoff (a test cutoff that is adjusted based on the reliability of the test) should be set by averaging the Angoff ratings given by job experts. Raters whose ratings are statistically different from other raters should be identified (by evaluating rater reliability and high/low rater bias) and removed.

Step 7: Post-Administration Analyses

Following the administration of the job-knowledge written test, conduct an item-level analysis of the test results to evaluate the item-level qualities (such as the point biserial, difficulty level, and DIF of each item as described in Chapter 6).

After conducting the item-level analysis and removing items that do not comply with acceptable ranges, conduct a test-level analysis to assess descriptive and psychometric statistics (such as reliability and Standard Deviation [SD]). After removing any test items with poor psychometric properties (sometimes due to incorrect keying), determine the final cutoff for the test by subtracting one, two, or three Standard Error of Measurements (SEMs) or Conditional SEMs (CSEMs) from the unmodified Angoff level.[15]

In summary, developing a content-valid, job-knowledge written test for hiring or promoting employees (where the job requires testing for critical job-knowledge areas) is the safest route to avoid potential litigation. If the test has adverse impact, it should be validated. Pay particular attention to address the Uniform Guidelines, Principles, and Standards (in that order, based on the weight they are typically given in court), and remember that a test is only as strong as its foundation. Be sure to base everything on a solid job analysis.

Steps for Developing a Personality Test Using Criterion-Related Validity

This section outlines the basic steps for developing and validating a low–adverse impact personality assessment for organizations that have at least two hundred and fifty incumbents in a specific job title or job group.

One of the most important human performance factors is personality. People's overall job performance can suffer due to personality, which is separate and distinct from intelligence or ability, and includes such traits as drive, initiative, focus, determination, and conscientiousness. Workers who are deficient in some of these characteristics will often fall short in a variety of job performance areas, such as: maintaining productive professional relationships, effectively solving interpersonal conflicts that arise with other coworkers or clients, staying focused on projects, and/or completing quality work.

How can human resource (HR) professionals identify these personality factors in the hiring and selection process? Conducting in-depth interviews can provide some insight into these areas as well as evaluating work history and patterns, but these types of investigations often require more time than HR professionals have. Further, HR professionals in mid- to large-sized organizations often screen hundreds and sometimes thousands of job candidates, making such in-depth investigations less than feasible. This is where written personality assessments play an integral role in the hiring process. Many personality measures are brief, succinct, and effective, but which traits are needed for the jobs in your organization? How can a valid personality test be developed for your organization? These questions and others will be answered in this brief how-to guide for developing validated personality tests.

Before proceeding, two issues should be stated. First, personality measures are a great way to lower adverse impact in most hiring processes because personality tests typically have less than half of the adverse impact commonly generated by cognitive ability tests.[16] Second, that being said, cognitive ability tests should not be removed from the process for the sole reason of avoiding possible adverse impact because they are typically solid predictors of job success. The ideal selection process is one that proportionately measures most of the key qualification factors needed for job success, including cognitive ability and personality.

Personality tests come by many different names. Some are called "work-style" tests, some are referred to as "profiles," and others as "personality measures." This section focuses on true, inherent personality factors, rather than attitudes and values that are sometimes more changeable over time.

By way of a disclaimer, test development is technical work. It requires statistical, psychological, and measurement knowledge and skills. Therefore, the following steps should be completed with great diligence, caution, thoroughness, and oversight.

Step 1: Research the Personality Traits That Underlie Job Performance

Literature searches can be conducted for the specific positions and the existing personality tools and traits that have efficiently predicted job success. For example, if the targeted personality area is "customer service orientation," the existing tools that measure this trait can be reviewed and their technical manuals reviewed to provide insight into what specific personality dimensions may translate to job success (copyright cautions are duly noted for this step). Personnel psychology literature should also be consulted to investigate the specific aspects of customer service orientation that have been associated with job success. Such research might identify that several aspects of customer-service orientation should be targeted for test development, such as sociability, extroversion, tactfulness, cooperativeness, flexibility, openness, optimism, and reliability.

At a minimum, the "Big Five" personality model should be evaluated and relevant aspects included (Barrick and Mount, 1991). Developed through years of study, it is considered to be the most comprehensive empirical or data-driven framework of personality currently available and includes five broad constructs, or dimensions, of personality: Openness, Conscientiousness, Extroversion, Agreeableness, and Neuroticism (the Neuroticism factor is sometimes referred to as Emotional Stability). Careful research may identify that some levels of one or more of these traits may be relevant for your targeted position(s).

Step 2: Develop a Bank of Test Items That Measure the Targeted Traits

Items should consist of short, behaviorally-based statements that are rated by the candidates on four levels of endorsement (1 = Strongly Disagree, 2 = Disagree, 3 = Agree, and 4 = Strongly Agree). For example, statements such as, "I am always prepared," "I like order," and "I pay attention to details" are examples of items that measure conscientiousness. In addition to positively-framed items (items in which higher endorsements mean the test taker is more likely to possess the targeted trait), negatively-framed items should also be included to make the construct of interest more obscure to the applicants who tend to "fake good" on personality tests (meaning they answer the way they feel will make them look best rather than responding honestly). For measuring conscientiousness, this might mean including items such as, "I leave my belongings around," or "Sometimes wrapping up the little details of a project is just a waste of time." In other words, measuring the inverse of a targeted trait is a subtle way to attempt to ensure that applicants are less able to intentionally misrepresent themselves on a personality test. For example, if one is developing a personality test for a public relations position and extroversion is thought to be a correlate of job success, measure introversion. Ultimately, the goal is to generate an item pool that is representative of both the low and high levels of each targeted trait. After the items have been developed, have them critiqued by an expert and reduced to a useable number (between one hundred and two hundred, with at least twenty measuring each targeted trait or dimension of that trait).

At this stage, it may also be beneficial to consider integrating items and/or scales from existing personality tests (e.g., one or more of the Big Five personality scales). Some test publishers are likely to negotiate license arrangements that will allow this.

Step 3: Develop a Lie Scale to Detect Faking and/or Random Responders

In nearly every criterion validation project, "random," "dishonest," and/or "illegitimate" responders exist and can wreak havoc on the study. One strategy to prevent this from happening is to develop ten to fifteen "lie-scale" items to be used for detecting and eliminating such responders. Lie scales can have contrasting pairs of items where the first is worded, "I like dogs more than cats," and the second is worded, "I like cats more than dogs" (for actual test items, use trait-relevant content). These sets can then be checked during the data analysis process and the non-matching responders can be excluded.

Step 4: Develop a Job Performance Rating Survey (JPRS)

This is one of the most important parts of the process because this is where the "target" (job performance) is created for the "arrows" (test items). Without a clear target, test items are meaningless. The Job Performance Rating Survey (JPRS) should be developed by working with job experts and reviewing the job description (or even better, a job analysis) to determine the important aspects of job behavior that are key for success in the target position. Select between ten and twenty different aspects of work behavior that are observable. Be sure not to double up in the same areas—it is better that each rating domain be as unique as possible.

To help maximize the likelihood of success, use a rating scale for each dimension that creates a distribution of the job incumbents that will be rated by supervisors. For example, the rating scale and instructions can advise the raters to divide their employees into ten (relatively) equal categories with about 10% of the employees in each. It should be explained to raters that assigning some of their employees to the lower 10%, 20%, or 30% categories does not mean that they are incompetent performers, but rather that this is where they stand in this single performance area, relevant to the rest of the staff. Completing a rating process in this way helps maximize the range of ratings obtained in the study and will allow for test items with greater levels of variance with which to correlate. Not completing the study in this fashion and using, for example, annual performance review scores can translate into the failure of the study. This can happen because such performance criteria can sometimes be influenced by political or emotional factors rather than objective observations that are relative to the job performance areas of the personality test in the study. These criteria are also sometimes too universal to be detected by the specific areas measured by the test. When selecting job performance criteria to include in the study, it is best to be specific as well as accurate (which means obtaining honest, candid, and widely varying job performance ratings).

Step 5: Convene the Supervisory Staff to Complete the JPRS on at Least 150 Target Incumbents

Be sure to conduct training and/or provide clear rating instructions to the supervisors. These instructions should explain that the ratings will be used exclusively for test-development purposes and will not be revealed to any outside agency. (Caution: It is recommended to first convince employee unions of the practical implications and confines of the study before attempting this process.) It is absolutely critical that the raters be encouraged to provide extremely candid and honest ratings through this process. If possible, have at least two supervisors rate each employee.[17] Employees should only be rated if they have at least one month of on-the-job experience and have been directly observed by the raters on each aspect of performance that is rated.

Step 6: Administer the Personality Test Items to the Target Incumbents

This step is relatively straightforward. The job incumbents should be informed that they are participating in a validation study that will be used for developing an assessment for selecting qualified workers (in the future). It should also be stressed that their test results will in no way be used for evaluating their personal job performance or pay status.

Step 7: Choose a Strategic Test Building Strategy

At this point, there are three possible strategies that can be used for evaluating the validity of the items included in the study and developing the test. The first (and most recommended) strategy is to use a two-step ("calibrate" and then "validate") process that is completed by dividing the total sample in half. One data set will be used to build the test (called the calibration sample); the other will be used to validate the test (called the validation sample). This process is called a split-half/hold-out validation. This process allows for the best possible test to be built, based specifically on the item-JPRS correlations observed in the calibration sample, and then trying this test out on the validation sample. This process is described in the remainder of this section. But first, two alternative methods are highlighted:

1. Factor analysis can be used on the entire sample of test takers to build test scales that can be correlated to the JPRS dimensions to evaluate statistically significant correlations. Either factor scoring (where each item is proportionally and positively/negatively weighted by its correlation to the factor) or manual item-factor weighting can be used to evaluate the correlation of test scales. Manual weighting can be done by identifying items that are above a certain item-factor correlation threshold (e.g., .20) and assigning them point values

according to their correlation strength to the factor (e.g., items with correlations >.30 are weighted 2X, above .20 weighted 1X, items with <.-30 weighted -2X, items with <.20 weighted -1X).

2. Test items can be sorted by construct (e.g., by grouping the conscientiousness items together, the extroversion items together, etc.) and evaluated for validity against the entire sample using a one-tailed test for significance (because they are based on a directional hypothesis for the correlation).

There are several caveats, conditions, and strengths/limitations with each of these strategies. The reader is advised to seek guidance where necessary. The following steps only discuss the split-half/hold-out (calibration/validation) study design.

Step 8: Set Up a Database for Conducting Correlational Analyses

First, evaluate and remove study participants who are deemed illegitimate using the Lie Scale (judgment must be used for determining just how many subjects to screen out and which decision rules are to be used prior to testing). Then, join the data files into a single database that contains each person's (raw, unscored) response on the test items and their ratings given by supervisors. Next, randomly divide the entire sample of incumbents into two equal data sets.

Step 9: Create the Optimal Test Using the Calibration Sample Only

Using the calibration sample only, run correlations between each test item and each of the dimensions on the JPRS, looking for correlational trends and patterns. If the JPRS has several differing areas (as might be shown through a factor analysis), some items may correlate with certain aspects of job performance but not others. This is where the art of test development comes in and advice from seasoned professionals becomes valuable.

After determining the items and dimensions on the JPRS that exhibit the strongest correlational trends, assign point values to the items that somewhat mirror their correlation strength. Important note: For this step, it is not necessary to select items that are only statistically significant. If an item demonstrates a positive correlational trend (say, >.20 or so) with one or more JPRS dimensions of interest, it should be selected for inclusion on the test and weighted appropriately. For example, if some items are found to exhibit high correlations across most JPRS dimensions, these items can be double weighted. For keying purposes, if items are negatively correlated with job performance, they should be reverse scored by assigning the highest point value to the lowest level of endorsement (rather than assigning the highest point value to the highest level of endorsement). Double weighting the strongest items will also help. This process will likely reduce the item pool by more than half.

After the new test form has been constructed, assess the reliability to be sure that the test overall (or each separate, scored subscale) has internal reliability that exceeds .70.[18] Because this process capitalizes on the sample-specific nuances that are inherent with the calibration sample, the total test will show an inflated correlation to the job performance dimensions and will probably exceed correlation values of .30 or .40. These values will not constitute the actual validity of the test; rather, they are inflated estimates. The actual test validity cannot be known until the next step has been completed.

Step 10: Evaluate the Validity of the Test by Correlating It to the JPRS Dimensions on the Hold-Out Validation Sample

Use only the validation sample (the other half of the data set that was not used for building the test in the step above) to correlate the test to the JPRS dimensions. Observed correlations that exceed statistical significance levels should be flagged for the steps that follow. Caution should be taken against trying too many correlations or retaining correlations that are barely significant, especially if they have adverse impact. In addition, an iterative process of going back and forth between the calibration and validation samples and data manipulation is strongly discouraged.

Step 11: Conduct a Fairness Study to Evaluate Whether the Test Is an Adequate Predictor of Job Success for Various Subgroups

Section 14B8 of the Uniform Guidelines requires conducting a fairness study whenever it is technically feasible to do so. Generally, this means that whenever a study includes at least thirty minorities or women, a fairness study should be conducted. This requires using Moderated Multiple Regression (MMR) to test for slope and intercept differences observed in the regression equations for the included subgroups (contact BCG[19] for a copy of a step-by-step guide for using MMR to evaluate test fairness). In addition to using MMR to evaluate the overall fairness of the test, Differential Item Function (DIF) analyses can be used for evaluating test fairness at the test item level (BCG also maintains the recommended steps, procedures, and tools for conducting DIF analyses, which are available at no charge).

Step 12: Assemble the Test and Determine the Appropriate Use in the Hiring Process

How the test is used in the hiring process (e.g., pass/fail, ranked, banded, or weighted and combined with other tests—see Chapter 6) should be based upon the validity, reliability, and adverse impact levels exhibited. Because personality tests typically have moderate levels of validity (high teens to mid-twenties) as well as reliability (hovering in the seventies/eighties), but typically have lower levels of adverse impact (when compared to, for instance, cognitive ability tests), banding is a good place to start (using the CSEM when setting score bands is recommended).[20] In addition, it is useful to add a warning to the test introductory page to help discourage applicant faking, such as: "It is important that you answer these questions as honestly and openly as possible. Failure to do so will likely result in a lower overall score. Some questions are worth more than one point, and some questions are scored in ways that would not be expected. Intentional deception is likely to result in lower overall performance."

Step 13: Complete a Criterion-Related Validation Report to Address Section 15B of the Uniform Guidelines

Completing a validation report that addresses the federal Uniform Guidelines provides three great benefits: (1) It provides a ready, off-the-shelf document that can be used in litigation situations; (2) it documents the key steps that were followed to build the test; and (3) it gives the test longevity. Tests that have no such pedigree can be minimized or disregarded over time, especially if the key personnel involved in their creation have left the organization. Tests that have a pedigree will maintain their value through time and turnover.

In summary, including a good personality test in your organization's hiring process is a great idea. The returns can be enormous anytime HR professionals can add validity and utility into their hiring process while reducing adverse impact. Following the key steps described above demonstrates how relatively easy it is to develop such a valuable asset.

Chapter 4—Structured Interviews

Developing, Validating, and Analyzing Structured Interviews

The purpose of any selection interview is to provide an applicant with a fair opportunity to demonstrate the KSAPCs and experiences that qualify him or her for the position. While interviews are the most commonly used component of selection systems, they can also be the most misunderstood and misapplied. Handled poorly, an interview may not only be ineffective, but may also cause unintended adverse impact. Otherwise qualified applicants may be eliminated if the many variables contributing to a successful interview are not properly implemented.

Because an interview, by nature, will not measure characteristics of the entire applicant, it should be used in conjunction with other selection procedures such as written exams or PATs. Using a structured interview can serve as a beneficial supplement to the other selection procedures and allow the employer to gain valuable insight regarding certain aspects of an applicant's KSAPCs. They are different from unstructured interviews in that the same questions are asked of every applicant, and in the same way, to ensure that all applicants are assessed using the same criteria.

Methods for Improving the Interview Process

It is important that an interview be as job-related as possible to ensure that the best applicants are hired as well as to avoid possible litigation. The following observations of typical interviews are both instructive and cautionary; they should be closely considered when developing an interview process:

- How valid and reliable the interview is may be highly specific to both the situation and to the rater.
- The interview should be used to evaluate factors that are not typically better measured by other means.
- The use of the interview is best accomplished if a standardized, or structured, approach is followed. In an unstructured interview, material is not consistently covered.
- The rater should be trained in eliciting full and complete responses from the applicant and synthesizing all of the information obtained.
- Even when a panel of raters obtains the same information, each panel member can interpret or weigh the information differently. It is best to use mechanically

combined scoring systems that consider several dimensions (rather than broad, sweeping, holistic judgments or ratings).

- The form of the question(s) affects the answer(s) obtained.

- The raters' attitudes affect their interpretations of what an applicant says.

- Raters appear to be influenced more by unfavorable, rather than favorable, information.

- Rapport, or the lack thereof, between rater and the applicant is a situational variable that can unduly influence the interview's effectiveness.

- Structured or patterned interviews show stronger inter-rater reliabilities, meaning that there is generally a greater agreement across different raters when a standardized interview is used.

- Raters typically develop stereotypes of a good/poor applicant and seek to match applicants with stereotypes.

- Biases are established by raters early in the interview and these tend to be followed by a bias-matching favorable or unfavorable decision.

- Raters seek data to support or deny their own personal hypotheses by focusing on information that supports their preconceived notions about applicants and dismissing information that does not.

While many of the characteristics of interviews are unfortunately beyond the control of the practitioner, two variables can be controlled: the amount of structure provided for the interview and the content of the interview. A structured interview is controlled by:

1. the interview questions asked (content);
2. the way the rater controls the actual interview situation (structure); and,
3. the standardized scoring of the interviews.

The remaining section will explain the various question types that can be included in an interview and provide a detailed, step-by-step process for developing and administering effective, valid, and structured interviews.

Types of Questions to Include in Structured Interviews: Situational, Behavioral, and Competency-Based

There is an entire landscape of question types that can be asked legally and effectively during an interview process. Some are more effective than others and, as a general rule, the more time and preparation invested in developing the question set, the better the questions and interviews will be. The following three basic question types will be covered: situational, behavioral, and competency-based.

Situational Questions

Situational questions often start by asking, "What would you do if …?" The best situational questions are typically based on critical incidents that have previously occurred (or are likely to occur) in the target position and ask the applicant to explain how he or she would handle that situation (possibly limited, of course, by not having previous experience in the position). Situational questions are a powerful selection tool in that they give the applicant an opportunity to draw upon past experience and demonstrate their decision-making abilities, or lack thereof. Most importantly, situational questions typically have good validity coefficients when correlated with measures of job performance (about .30 to .46), as well as solid reliability (inter-rater reliability estimates are typically between .76 and .87) (Gatewood, 1994; and Cascio, 1998). Consider the following example from an electrical trade position:

> Workers at XYZ Company have a practice of checking tools for proper operation prior to leaving the shop to go to a job site. This allows workers to be assured that tools will work properly at the job site. Your supervisor asks you to work with three helpers to collect and test the tools that will be brought to the next job site. After the helpers assist you in gathering and testing the tools, the tools are loaded in the truck and brought to the work site. After starting work at the site, your supervisor finds that one of the tools that you and the three helpers loaded is not working properly. He gets angry and demands that you drive all the way back to the shop to obtain a new tool. You know which one of the helpers gave you the faulty tool. What would you do in this situation? What would you expect to accomplish by taking these steps?

Typically, for situational questions of this type, scoring guidelines and anchors that provide benchmarks to raters for high, acceptable, and low levels of applicant responses are developed prior to interview administration.

Behavioral Questions

Behavioral questions ask applicants: "What have you done when …?" These questions are based on the reasonable assumption that the best predictor of future behavior is past behavior. As such, these questions ask applicants to explain how they have handled difficult or complex situations in previous settings. Generally speaking, these questions are the most limited type of interview questions since they can sometimes be faked with information the interviewer has no way of confirming. The following is an example of a behavioral series:

> It is sometimes necessary to work as part of a team to accomplish a project. Can you tell me about a time during a job or school project

where you were part of a team and one or more of the members were difficult to work with? Please explain how you handled this situation. What was the outcome? Would you do anything differently now?

Competency-Based Questions

Competency-based questions ask applicants: "Explain how you would …" This question type drills deep into the applicant's knowledge and skill set in a way that leaves little room for impression management or faking. When properly developed, administered, and scored, these questions are one of the most powerful selection tools for complex jobs that require high levels of knowledge and skill upon entry.

Consider an information technology (IT) management position. IT managers need to possess good interpersonal and project management skills, but most importantly, they need to possess solid, mastery-level knowledge and skills relevant to the computer systems they will be managing. Asking only situational and behavioral type questions when interviewing for this position is almost certainly a recipe for disaster (unless the situational questions include competency-based characteristics). It is entirely possible during an interview that asks only situational and behavioral questions to completely miss whether the IT manager applicant possesses the mastery-level knowledge and skill necessary to actually perform the job. An example of a competency-based question for the IT manager position might be:

> Our company has thirty-five employees and we use Microsoft® Mail Server version XX.0 for our email services. If Microsoft released a new version of the Mail Server program next month, what steps would you take to migrate our company to the new version? Please be specific and be sure to describe each step you would take and why. Feel free to take your time to prepare your answer before responding.

After the applicant has provided his or her complete response, ask additional follow-up questions (to be asked of every applicant), such as:

- How would you notify staff of the change?
- What backup plans would you have in place before starting the work?
- When would you start the project?
- What problems have you had with Mail Server Version XX.0?
- What do you like about Mail Server Version XX.0?
- What steps would you follow to set up a new employee's mail account?
- What books or reference sources would you consult before or during the migration process?

While the situational and behavioral questions can help evaluate how the applicant will likely work with people and handle projects, such questions may completely overlook the depth and breadth of an applicant's true computer-related knowledge and skill. Including some solid, competency-based questions into the mix of other questions addresses this problem.

Questions of this type pose a challenging hurdle for unqualified applicants to overcome, especially when coupled with follow-up questions and scored by IT professionals who are familiar with the topics covered in the interview. Generally speaking, competency-based and follow-up questions can be even more specific than the examples above (more specific questions are better, provided that the question does not measure knowledge that will be trained on the job).

Steps for Developing Situational Questions

The following is a detailed description of the steps necessary for developing validated situational questions for a structured interview.

1. Complete a job analysis for the target position. Be sure that the job analysis includes (at a minimum) duties, KSAPCs, linkages between the duties and KSAPCs (required to address Section 14C4 of the Guidelines), and Best-Worker ratings (see the job analysis ratings discussed in Chapter 3). Each of these steps should be performed before proceeding further in the development process.

2. Select the KSAPCs to measure at the interview by following the steps for completing a selection plan outlined in Chapter 3. Be sure that the KSAPCs that are selected for the interview can be appropriately measured in an interview format (for example, KSAPCs such as reading ability, math, and practical types of skills cannot usually be properly assessed by an interview and are typically better assessed using other methods). Also, be sure that the KSAPCs selected for the interview are performance differentiating (rated highest on the Best-Worker rating scale). This is helpful, especially if the interview will be used as the final, ranked, or banded selection procedure.

3. Prepare for a one-day workshop with job experts by compiling a final list of the selected KSAPCs and create a Situational Interview Question form. This form should provide space for the job experts to record a critical incident (see below) that has occurred on the job (or likely could occur), the KSAPC that is related to that incident, and the least effective, acceptable, and most effective responses to the situation.

4. Convene seven to ten job experts for the one-day workshop to draft situational questions for the interview. Start the workshop by explaining the work

completed so far (e.g., the job analysis, selecting KSAPCs for the interview), the benefits of using a job-related interview process (it helps to specifically mention that the end goal of the process is to effectively select new employees for the job who will be excellent coworkers), and the final product—a valid structured interview.

5. Break the job experts into two to three groups (each having at least two individuals) with each team having roughly the same number of KSAPCs (e.g., if there are twelve KSAPCs that survived the selection plan screening process above, divide the job experts into four teams with each having three KSAPCs). Have each team review its set of KSAPCs and the duties to which they are linked. This will re-familiarize the job experts with the KSAPCs and how they are specifically applied on the job.

6. Review the concept of critical incidents with the job experts. Spend some time with the concept, asking for group input and examples of critical incidents that have occurred on the job, or likely could.

7. The critical incidents should not include common, everyday events. The best critical incident is one where the words and actions of the incumbent would directly translate into a positive or negative outcome with regard to an important aspect of the job.

8. Prepare the panel for developing situational questions based on these critical incidents by reviewing the criteria presented below. The situational question should:

   a. not measure KSAPCs that an employee will be expected to learn on the job, or can be trained in a brief orientation. That is, the question should not penalize applicants who have a high level of the KSAPC being measured by the question, but are unable to respond with much information to the question because they do not have experience in the target position.

   b. provide sufficient content and complexity to stimulate a response from the applicant that would allow raters to provide an adequate assessment of the applicant. Situations that have simple solutions or present only absolute alternatives should be avoided.

   c. be job-related (it should represent an incident that has occurred, or is very likely to occur on the job).

   d. not be too easy or too difficult.

   e. be culturally and politically sensitive and appropriate. In other words, it should present a situation that allows qualified applicants of various socio-ethnic backgrounds to provide ample responses.

9. Ask the individual team members to independently develop critical incidents that relate to their assigned KSAPCs. Remind them that critical incidents can include situations that have occurred on the job (to them or someone else) or would be very likely to occur. Ask the job experts to record these incidents on the Situational Interview Question Form. Be sure they complete all parts of the survey. It sometimes helps to do the first one as an example with the overall group. Ask each job expert to come up with at least four incidents. Allow ample time for this process.

   a. Have the job experts exchange their completed forms and ask each team to refine the incidents within its team and select the best ones. If there are three team members and each job expert developed four incidents (for a total of twelve), the team might select a final set of eight of their best incidents.

10. Have the job experts submit the incidents and read each one (without revealing the author of the incident) to the entire group. Have the group informally grade each one with traditional scholastic ratings of A, B, or C.

11. Keep the incidents that were graded A or B by the group. Use the following steps to convert the incidents into final situational questions:

   a. Convert the incidents into question form to be asked directly of the applicant (e.g., "Assume you are a clerical worker at XYZ corporation and the following event occurs …").

   b. Refine the possible responses (least effective, acceptable, and most effective) to include typical responses that applicants are likely to provide during the interview. This step is important because these response guidelines will be used in the interview scoring process.

   c. Develop customized follow-up questions for each situational question. These follow-up questions are useful for escalating the situation, in a standardized format, for applicants who initially provide superficial responses for how they would address the situation.

12. Develop a final interview package that includes the final situational questions along with standardized rating forms and scoring summary forms (to be used to compile scores from individual raters to the panel as a whole). Because practical judgment, decision making, and verbal communication are measured inclusively along with each situational question, they can be scored for each situational question or in terms of the overall performance of the applicant (after answering all questions).

13. It is possible to conclude at this step with a set of situational questions that are highly job-related and will effectively screen applicants for relevant KSAPCs. However, an additional step can be included in the process at this point that will have two benefits: (1) it will generate validation evidence and documentation should the interview ever be challenged, and (2) it can refine the final set of questions to be even better than the initial set. This step involves convening a team of seven to ten job experts (who have not yet seen the final set of situational questions) to review and provide validation ratings for the situational questions. This step is beneficial from a practical standpoint because it serves to provide a fresh perspective on the situational questions as the final product is reviewed by job experts who have never seen them. This step is best executed by having the new team of job experts evaluate the set of situational questions using the following ratings:

   a. Is the question clear and understandable?

   b. Is the question written at an appropriate level of difficulty?

   c. Does the question measure a KSAPC that is needed the first day of the job?

   d. Is the question fair to all groups of people?

   e. Is the question job-related? (Does it represent a situation that has occurred or is very likely to occur on the job?)

   f. What KSAPC is measured by the question?

   g. Will applicants be able to provide a sufficient response without possessing job-specific (or employer-specific) knowledge?

The court-endorsed rating guidelines for written tests, presented in Chapter 3, can be readily adopted as criteria for selecting a valid set of situational questions.

Administering and Scoring an Interview

The steps below can be followed to administer and score an interview in a fair and defensible manner:

1. Select raters to serve on interview panels. Raters can be supervisors of the target position and/or human resource staff members. If high-level knowledge is required, competency-type questions will be used and knowledge of the subject matter is essential for raters (in many instances, this will necessitate using supervisors only).

2. Train the raters on the questions, scoring forms, and common rating errors. The following rating errors should be explained and demonstrated to raters:

a. Halo: Halo refers to the tendency of the rater to rate an applicant in about the same way on all domains because of a general, overall impression—whether favorable or unfavorable. This error usually results because the rater becomes impressed, either favorably or unfavorably, with one or two of the qualification areas and tends to base ratings in all qualification areas according to this initial impression.

b. Leniency: This error refers to the tendency of raters to place their ratings in the higher end of the scale for all applicants. This error occurs mainly because raters often feel that placing everyone in the top categories is helpful or kind. In actuality, it can render ratings useless.

c. Severity: This error refers to the tendency for raters to put a greater proportion of their ratings in categories below the average than in those above.

d. Central Tendency: This error is very common in the rating situation. It refers to the tendency of the rater to place all ratings at the center of the scale. This may occur because the rater is not entirely clear as to the meaning of the ratings or perhaps wishes to play it safe by giving no extreme ratings in either direction. Of course, this results in little or no variability between applicants and thus detracts from the objectives of the interview. This can also render the ratings useless.

e. Similar-to-Me: This type of rating error occurs when certain characteristics about the applicant bias the scores up, or high, when they are similar to the rater and down, or low, when they are not.

3. Assemble panels and randomly assign applicants to panel members. Rating panels should consist of at least three members and preferably no more than six. Two-member panels are also plausible, but detecting rater bias is limited when only two raters are used. If possible, ensure that the panels are diverse with respect to ethnicity and gender.

4. Administer and score the interview. After the scores are compiled, they should be double-checked for accuracy.

5. If multiple rater panels are used and each panel rates more than twenty applicants (or so), standard score each panel before combining all applicant scores onto the final score list. Standard scoring can be accomplished by creating a Z score for each applicant by subtracting each applicant's score from the average (mean) score of all applicants rated by the panel and dividing this value by the panel's SD (of all applicant total scores on that panel). Only after completing this step for each panel should the applicant scores be combined and ranked on a final score list. This process statistically equates applicant

scores between panels (sometimes rater panels have higher or lower averages for applicant scores and this process places them on the same level).[21]

Chapter 5—Developing Valid Work-Sample Physical Ability Tests (PATs)

Public safety occupations are generally physically demanding. Departments often struggle with the task of developing and implementing defensible testing instruments that can select candidates who will succeed in the physical aspects of jobs within the public safety sector.

For example, some fire departments institute stringent cardiovascular fitness tests that use stair climbing machines or stationary bicycles to estimate the applicant's maximum V02 threshold.[22] Such tests may lead to disgruntled applicants who feel the test lacks face validity because they do not perceive a direct connection between the level of the test and the requirements of the job, which can lead to low perceptions of fairness. In addition, if a test is too rigorous, it could be considered a test that measures an applicant's "physiological or biological responses to performance" and would then be classified (by the EEOC under the Americans with Disabilities Act [ADA] of 1990) as a medical examination, which means that it can only be administered after a contingent job offer has been made.[23] Additionally, the scoring and use of this type of test becomes even more challenging because the scoring formulas typically require using gender and age (Siconolfi, Garber, Lasater, and Carleton, 1985), which is a specific violation of the 1991 Civil Rights Act with regard to employment testing.[24]

Other departments institute only static strength tests that measure whether an applicant is capable of lifting or manipulating the weights that are routinely handled on the job and leave stamina unmeasured in the hiring process. Still other departments do not install any form of physical testing and leave it to chance as to whether candidates will be able to perform rigorous job requirements. None of these solutions alone will likely serve the department's best interests when hiring for a physically-demanding job.

The best way to ensure that candidates are physically job-ready is to develop a test that replicates vital activities of the position. In this way, whatever combination of strength and fitness that is required for the actual job is mirrored on the pre-employment test (as much of each that can feasibly be included on a pre-employment test). Research strongly suggests there will be fewer dissatisfied test takers if the content of a test is transparently similar to the content of the job, such that those who fail the test would realize that they probably would not have successfully performed the job. Applicants typically perceive work-sample tests as being more fair than other types of tests because they look and feel like the actual job. Such tests also result in fewer applicants walking away disgruntled from their testing experience, even if they fail the test.

With that in mind, it is frequently helpful if the content and context of this type of test (called a work-sample or PAT) mimics critical or important work behaviors that constitute most of the job. In the words of Section 14C4 of the Guidelines, "the closer the content and context of the selection procedure are to work samples or work behaviors, the stronger is the basis for showing content validity." The following is a description of a content-related validity strategy for creating and validating a PAT.

Steps for Developing a PAT Using Content Validity

Step 1: Conduct a Thorough Job Analysis that Focuses on the Physical Aspects of the Job

Identify the parts of the job (e.g., job duties or sets of job duties) that are typically performed in rapid succession and collectively require continuous physical exertion for over ten minutes. This can include one job duty repeatedly performed where a rapid work pace is required on the job (e.g., loading or unloading a fire hose for firefighter positions), or a set of unrelated job duties where a rapid pace is required for physically demanding job duties (e.g., pulling hoses and then raising the fly section of a ladder).

Step 2: Work with Supervisors and Trainers to Assemble a Continuously-Timed, Multiple-Event Work-Sample PAT

The PAT events included need to be those where a rapid (but safe) working pace is important. If you wish to use physical ability testing for parts of the job that are not typically performed in rapid succession, then work with supervisors and trainers to assemble test events for measuring the ability to perform those parts of the job.

Any pace, distance, weights, or other limitations used during testing must be job-related (related to actual pace, distances, weights, or other limitations that are required on the job). For example, if an employee would have up to three minutes to move something from point A to point B on the job, then the candidate should not be required to perform this same task in less time during the test.[25] Similarly, if an employee is expected to carry an object a certain distance on the job, but is allowed to briefly place that object on the ground to rest and/or change his or her grip, the test taker should also be allowed to rest and/or change his or her grip if required to carry an item during a test, in a similar manner. In other words, the test should be similar in difficulty and execution to the actual job and should not require the test taker to carry more weight, move something a longer distance, or perform work that is substantially more difficult than on the actual job.

Test events that mimic work behaviors do not require a statistical examination of test performance and job performance to be conducted. Alternatively, test events that do not mimic work behaviors, but which are predictive of job performance, can be used if a statistically significant relationship can be shown between performance on the test and performance on the job. To use this type of testing, a relatively large number of job candidates or current employees (at least one hundred and fifty is recommended, though meaningful studies can be conducted with smaller samples if the relationship between the test and job performance is relatively strong) must take the test and their test scores should be statistically compared to their work performance. This process utilizes a criterion-related validation strategy described on the next page.

Step 3: Run a Representative Random Sample of Job Experts (typically at least twenty to thirty) through the PAT and Administer a Validation Survey That Collects the Following Information:

1. Actual PAT completion time. If you are using a continuously-timed, multiple-event job simulation PAT, then collect the time it takes each job expert to complete all of the events combined. If you are using a single-event PAT, or a series of single-event PATs, then collect the time it takes each job expert to complete each test event. This information will be used for setting a job-related cutoff score—see the section titled "Selecting a Cutoff Time for an Applicant or Incumbent Work-Sample PAT."

2. Their yes or no answers to the following questions:

    a. Does the PAT measure skills/abilities that are important/critical (essential for the performance of the job)?

    b. Does the PAT fairly measure the applicant's natural abilities that are needed for the position on the first day, prior to training?

    c. Does the PAT replicate/simulate actual work behaviors in a manner, setting, and level of complexity similar to the job?

    d. Do the events in the PAT need to be completed on the job in a rapid and safe manner (is speed important)?

    e. Are the weights and distances involved in the PAT representative of the job?

    f. Is the duration that the objects/equipment are typically carried or handled in the PAT similar to what is required of a single person on the job?

    g. Is the PAT free from any special techniques that are learned on the job that allow current job incumbents to perform the PAT events better than an applicant could (that are not demonstrated to the applicants prior to taking the PAT)?

    h. Does the PAT require the same or less exertion of the applicant than is required on the job?

Step 4: Analyze the Job Expert Data Gathered from Step 3

First, analyze the yes/no ratings gathered from step 3, number 2c (above). At least 70% of the job experts must answer yes to each question. If this is not the case, go back to the drawing board and redesign the test as necessary. Then resurvey the job experts until at least 70% of the job experts endorse each one.

Steps for Developing a PAT Using Criterion-Related Validity

Step 1: Complete Steps 1–3 Outlined in the Preceding Content Validity Section

Step 2: Administer the PAT

If a concurrent criterion-related validation strategy (where the PAT will be administered to current job incumbents from the target position) will be used, administer the PAT to one hundred and fifty current incumbents. The benefit of conducting a concurrent study is that it is fast; the researcher will find out quickly if the PAT is valid (if it is significantly correlated to job performance). The drawback is that concurrent studies sometimes have less power than predictive studies (because of range restriction in the post-screened worker population involved in the study). This might result in a situation where the study does not reveal a significant correlation that actually exists in the greater population and would have shown up if a larger study had been conducted. Another drawback of a concurrent study is that it requires off-the-job time from incumbents to complete the PAT.

If a predictive criterion-related validation strategy (where the PAT will be administered to applicants and subsequently rated on job performance) will be used, administer the PAT to one hundred and fifty applicants who will be subsequently hired (e.g., five hundred tested, one hundred and fifty hired). One of the benefits of using a predictive study is that it may have higher power (increased likelihood of finding significance) because the employer is testing a broader ability range of applicants (compared to the post-tested employee group used in a concurrent study). Another advantage is that a predictive study is passive in that it does not take existing employees off the job. The drawback is that it takes time and resources to test and finally hire one hundred and fifty or more applicants who will need to subsequently be rated on job performance.

Step 3: Develop a Job Performance Rating Survey (JPRS)

The JPRS is to be used for gathering job-performance ratings (e.g., using a one-to-ten rating scale) from supervisors (and/or coworkers) for each incumbent who completed the PAT. Several aspects of job performance (e.g., five to ten) that are assumed to be related to the PAT scores should be included. A word of caution on this part of the study: Supervisors or coworkers are often hesitant to provide any of their team members with average or below-average ratings, and this tendency can easily impede the study because correlations are strongest when the low-, middle-, and high-performance ranges are represented (on both the test and the job performance sides of the study). For this reason, it is strongly advised to inform study participants that the performance ratings will only be used for test validation purposes.

Step 4: Administer the JPRS

Collect the ratings after administering the JPRS.

Step 5: Complete the Statistical Analyses

This step should be used to determine whether the PAT is significantly correlated to one or more job performance dimensions.

Selecting a Cutoff Time for an Applicant or Incumbent Work-Sample PAT

Taking the proper steps to develop validated cutoff scores for continuously-timed work-sample PATs, for both applicant (pre-hire) and incumbent (post-hire) populations, will help ensure both fairness and defensibility in court. Part of this process should specifically address the criteria in the Uniform Guidelines regarding the "normal expectations of acceptable proficiency" in the workforce (Section 5H) and other relevant criteria from federal and professional testing standards.

When it comes to setting cutoff scores that represent the normal expectations of acceptable proficiency in the workforce, it might seem natural to simply run a sample of incumbents through the PAT and set the cutoff score at the average time that it took incumbents to complete the test. There are several problems with this approach, the first being that such an approach would assume that about half of the workforce (those that scored below the average) performs inadequately.[26] There are four additional challenges that will be discussed in more detail in the following pages:

1. Possible ability and skill advantage of the incumbent workforce
2. Influential outliers
3. Sampling error
4. Test unreliability

Possible Skill Advantage of the Incumbent Workforce

The goal of a PAT used for screening entry-level applicants is to measure their ability to perform the requirements of the job at a level required on the first day of employment (before training or on-the-job experience, see Section 14C1 of the Guidelines). Measuring the performance levels of the current workforce can provide useful information on setting cutoff scores for untrained applicants, but not without some of the following complications:

1. The incumbent workforce with less than one year of experience can sometimes have higher *ability levels* on the work-sample tasks included on the test. This is due to their recent completion of the training academy (where some of the training is targeted at improving their underlying ability and fitness levels, as well as their job-specific skills). In many circumstances, this advantage is short-lived and is not continued through job tenure (unless it is sustained through ongoing physical training).

2. The incumbent workforce may possess *skill levels* that are higher than entry-level applicants, even if the applicants possess identical levels of the underlying abilities measured by the PAT. This may result from post-academy time on the job to practice the work behaviors that may be represented on the PAT. Although valid work-sample PATs should exclude test content that is "learned in a brief orientation" or "trained on the job" (these are two typical ratings in PAT content validation studies designed to address Section 14C1 of the Guidelines), it may not be possible to remove all skills and techniques that may give incumbents an advantage when completing the PAT. Even if the test is completely free of such content, there is still a possibility that incumbents, through their regular practice and application of the work behaviors that are similar to those represented on the test, may have an advantage. This "incumbent advantage" may be 1%, 5%, 10%, or higher, but is likely present at some level.

Influential Outliers

Most groups of incumbents selected to complete a PAT (especially when the purpose is to set a cutoff that will be used for setting a maintenance- or return-to-duty standard that will be applied to the same group) will typically include one or more exceptionally high and exceptionally low incumbent scores. These outlier scores have more influence on the mean and the variability of the sample because of how the underlying math works for computing both of these statistics. These outliers are sometimes referred to by statisticians as "influential data points" because they are outside of the normal range of the score distribution. For this reason, these outliers should be identified and removed from the data set using the process described in Step 2 later in this chapter.

Sampling Error

The average score that is derived from running the incumbent workforce through the PAT is subject to sampling error. Unless the entire workforce runs through the PAT, the average obtained from running the sample of incumbents through the test will be subject to natural variability that occurs around the central parts of the distribution. This sampling error (called the Standard Error of the Mean, or SE Mean) is 0 when the entire workforce runs through the PAT and increases in value when the sample selected is small (in an absolute sense) relative to the population from which it was chosen.

By definition, the SE Mean is the confidence interval that surrounds the average derived from the sample. For example, an average incumbent score of 300 seconds obtained from a sample of thirty incumbents (who were selected from a population of two hundred) with a SD of 30 seconds will have a SE Mean of 5.06 seconds (using the computations discussed below). This means that 68% of the additional samples of thirty incumbents that are drawn from this population of two hundred incumbents will likely produce average scores between 295 seconds and 305 seconds (5 seconds above/below the 300-second average obtained from the first draw of thirty incumbents). This variability produces uncertainty about the average obtained from the first sample draw, but can be accounted for by simply adding one SE Mean to the average time which provides 84% confidence that the population average is this time or less.

Test Unreliability

Every assessment device used in personnel testing produces scores that are less-than-perfect estimates of the examinee's true ability level measured by the test. Applicants who take a PAT are not exempt from this phenomenon, as they will achieve a different score almost every time they take the PAT. The best way to estimate this variability on a continuously-timed, work-sample PAT and develop a fixed confidence interval around such hypothetical repeat test scores is to administer the test twice to a group of incumbents (e.g., n > 50) and compute an ICC[27] (a type of reliability estimate for test-retest conditions) which can be combined with the SD of scores to produce a SEM using the formula:

$$\text{SEM} = \sigma_x \sqrt{1 - ICC}$$

Here σ_x is the SD of test scores (from the first administration, where examinees are less practiced), and ICC is the test-retest reliability coefficient of the test. For example, a test with an ICC = .70 and a SD = 50 would result in a SEM of 27.39 ($50\sqrt{1 - .70}$) (rounded to 27 for purposes of the hypothetical discussion below).

Much like the SD of test scores, the SEM can be used to estimate boundaries around test scores. However, in the case of the SEM, the boundaries pertain to an individual examinee's true score, given his or her observed score. Observed scores are simply that—the score that a certain examinee achieves. True scores, however, represent the score that most accurately represents the examinee's true, actual ability level (as represented by the test). The true score can also be regarded as the average score an examinee would achieve if he or she (hypothetically) completed the test a thousand times.

For example, an examinee who gets a score of 500 seconds on a first administration of the test (the observed score) likely has a true score of between 473 seconds and 527 seconds (one SEM of seconds below and above the observed score). This one-SEM boundary around the examinee's observed score encapsulates his or her true score with 68% certainty. Using two SEMs to establish this boundary sets the true score boundary with 95% certainty.

Because each examinee's true score has a 50% likelihood of existing at or below his or her observed score and a 50% likelihood of existing at or above his or her observed score, a researcher can determine the probability of an examinee's true score existing at a certain score or higher. This means that this examinee's true score is 84% likely to exist at or below a score of 527 seconds (the 500-second observed score plus one SEM (27 seconds) = 527 seconds). The 84% is determined by adding 34% (half of the 68% bidirectional boundary obtained using one SEM) to the 50% likelihood that his or her true score is lower than his or her observed score. Thus, the odds are about six-to-one ($1 \div 16\%$) that this examinee's true score is at or below 527 seconds.

The SEM can be multiplied by the square root of two to compute a Standard Error of Difference (SED), which is a metric that is useful for establishing a confidence interval between two scores. So, the SED is concerned with differentiating between the true scores of examinees given their observed scores, whereas the SEM identifies the range surrounding one examinee's true score given his or her observed score. Using the example above, the SED can be computed as: 27.39 * 1.41421 = 38.73.

After computing the SED, the SED can be multiplied by a confidence interval (e.g., 90%) to establish a specified degree of confidence regarding the distance (number of scores) above or below before reaching a score that represents a meaningfully different ability level. In other words, the SED can be used to identify two true scores that are reliably isolated in the score distributions so that the hypothetical repeat test scores of two examinees would not likely overlap. For example, multiplying the SED by 1.645 and adding this product to the average score sets the 95% limit for scores that are reliably within the normal upper range as marked by the average score. Using our example above, we arrive at this outside boundary score as: 500 seconds (average) + SED (38.73) * 95% Confidence Interval (1.645) = 63.71 = 564 seconds (rounded up).

Thus, applicants who score 564 seconds or faster are within the normal range (or faster), and applicants who score slower than 564 seconds are outside of this normal range and exist within an ability range that is meaningfully outside of the normal.

Setting Cutoff Scores for Applicants and Incumbents

The discussion above demonstrates that setting cutoff scores that equate with an acceptable level of proficiency in the workforce is not as easy as testing the incumbent workforce and simply using the average. Further, even using a simple descriptive statistic such as adding one SD to the average, would not address the four factors discussed above (the possible ability and skill advantage of the incumbent workforce, possible influential outliers, sampling error, and the unreliability that is inherent with the test).

The process described below shows how each of these factors can be integrated into a process for setting applicant and incumbent cutoff scores for a firefighter PAT. This discussion assumes that a content-validated, continuously-timed, work-sample PAT is being used. At a minimum, such a test should include events that are (as much as possible) free of techniques that are trained on the job (by either removing such techniques, teaching them to the applicants beforehand, or setting up the events so that the techniques are built into the testing process), and includes only events where speed (rapid, yet safe, movement) is important both within and between the events.

Step 1: Adjust for the Possible Gap between the Incumbent Workforce and the Applicant Population

One way of completing this step is to run active incumbents (typically captain and lower ranks) through the test, then have them complete a brief survey that asks their opinion regarding the time in which a minimally-qualified applicant (with no academy or job training) should be able to complete the test (see the Angoff method described in Biddle [2011]).

After the incumbents' actual and opinion times are tabulated, two results are very likely. First, their average actual and opinion times will be different, with slightly more time being afforded to the applicants. Second, a negative correlation will emerge between these two values and the time in which the incumbents completed the test. In other words, the fastest incumbents will likely extend more time (than their own time) to applicants, and the slowest incumbents will likely extend less time to the applicants. This phenomenon has occurred in every one of the numerous data sets that the authors have evaluated (pertaining to the fire service industry) and likely occurs because the exceptionally fit incumbents recognize that typical applicants may have less ability, and less fit incumbents may desire stronger ability levels of incoming applicants. Figure 5-1 demonstrates this graphically using data from a study that involved two hundred and fourteen firefighters from forty-one departments in a consortium study.

Figure 5-1. Difference between Firefighter Actual Time and Recommended Applicant Time

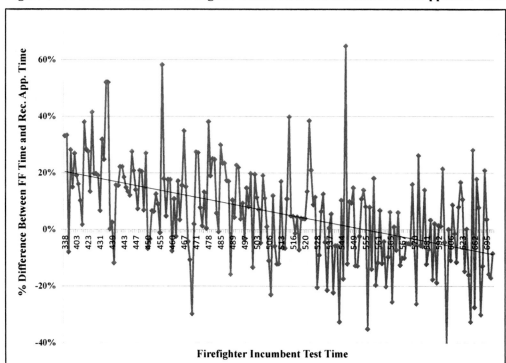

Given that this strong negative correlation exists between actual and recommended times (r = -0.462 in this study and even stronger in other studies),[28] regression can be used to identify adjustments that can be made at various score levels to account for the skill advantage that incumbents may possess. For example, Figure 5-1 shows that the predicted recommended applicant time is about 12% slower (506 seconds) for fast incumbents who score 443 seconds (one SD below the mean), about 5% slower (541 seconds) for incumbents who score at the mean (516 seconds), and 2% faster (576 seconds) for slower incumbents who score 589 seconds (one SD above the mean).

This data is useful because it can be used in a regression formula to predict the additional amount of time that should be given to applicants at various score levels in the incumbent population. For example, in one study[29] conducted by the authors, the applicant advantage score was computed to be 5.56% at the average score. Because this value represents the predicted opinion at the normal (average) point of the score distribution, it can be simply added to the incumbent average score to arrive at a starting place for computing the cutoff score for applicants (see additional steps required below).

Step 2: Remove the Outliers

This step is important because nearly every incumbent score distribution will have outliers, and these outliers may have a significant influence on cutoff scores due to the greater influence they can have on the average score used in the process of cutoff-score setting. There are a number of different methods available for trimming outliers, ranging from manual to automatic methods. While most methods will return similar results, one decision must be made surrounding the percentage of data points to trim, with the minimum being a 5% trim (where the lowest and highest 5% scores are removed, or 10% of the total) to a 20% trim. (Wilcox and Keselman, 2003)

Trimming the data can be done in several ways. The method we recommend for PAT scores is to remove the outliers from both the mean and SD because, if they are truly viewed as outliers (i.e., not representative of the normal score ranges that will be used for determining the cutoff score), they should be completely removed from the cutoff determination process. However, while trimming the outer regions of a distribution can lead to more accurate estimations of the true population mean, doing so can also suppress the variability around the mean (the SD) because the extreme data points contribute the most variance to such formulae.

For this reason, and because the SD is being used in this process to set boundaries regarding the normal expectations of acceptable proficiency, we suggest trimming the SD using 1.645 SD trimming rule, which only excludes 10% of the data (5% on each side). This is done by computing the mean and SD of the entire distribution, multiplying the SD by 1.645, and excluding the values that exceed this range (on both the high and low side). For example, given a mean of 500 seconds and a SD of 100 seconds, all scores below 335 seconds (500-(1.645*100)) and above 665 (500+(1.645*100)) would be removed from the dataset.

While a variety of procedures and methods may be useful for trimming outliers, the authors have found the process described above especially effective because the vast majority of incumbent datasets from incumbents have been significantly skewed (with a disproportionally high number of slower incumbents than faster incumbents in the dataset).[30]

Step 3: Correct for Sampling Error

The SE Mean can be computed using the following formula:

$$SD / \sqrt{N}$$

where SD is the SD of the untrimmed scores and N is the sample size. This value should be reduced by multiplying it by the Finite Population Correction (FPC)[31] value, computed by:

$$\sqrt{\frac{N-n}{N-1}}$$

where N is the total incumbent population and n is the sample included in the study.

Step 4: Account for Test Reliability

Compute an ICC statistic in SPSS® (Statistical Package for Social Sciences) by inserting Time 1 scores and Time 2 scores in their respective columns and analyzing the scale reliability using Intraclass Correlation Coefficient, Two-Way Mixed (with Absolute type), and using the Average Measures value from the resulting output. Then use the ICC to compute the SEM and finally the SED.

If possible, the test-retest reliability (ICC) for the entry-level PAT should be computed using untrained applicants or new recruits, and the ICC for the incumbent PAT should be computed using incumbent personnel. This is because the applicant reliability is likely to be lower than the incumbents, due to their having less on-the-job experience with the same or similar activities. For our example, the authors conducted a test-retest study with fifty-nine new fire recruits that resulted in ICC = 0.6979 (for a work-sample PAT that had an average time of about nine minutes) and a test-retest study for incumbents for a similar PAT that resulted with a higher ICC (ICC = 0.7927). Use the ICC from the untrained applicants in the cutoff process described below for the entry-level PAT, and the ICC from the incumbent PAT.

Step 5: Combine the Computation Values to Set Cutoff Scores for Entry-Level Applicants and Incumbents (as a Maintenance Standard)

Given the discussion of the factors and computations above, the following formulas can be used for computing passing scores (cutoffs) for entry-level applicants and incumbents (as a maintenance or return-to-duty standard):

Formula for Setting Cutoff Scores for Entry-Level Applicants:

Trimmed Mean + (Trimmed Mean * 5.56%) + (SE Mean * FPC) + (SED * 1.96)

Process for Setting Cutoff Scores for Incumbents (for a Maintenance or Return-to-Duty Standard):

Trimmed Mean + (SE Mean * FPC) + (SED * 1.96)

The final cutoff for either process above should be set by rounding the calculated value up to a whole second (e.g., 500.10 seconds should be rounded up to 501 seconds) because it is easier to monitor pass/fail determinations in whole seconds.

While the results of the process above will vary, the cutoffs will typically be set so that >90% of the incumbents would pass the applicant standard and 80% to 90% of the incumbents would pass the maintenance- or return-to-duty standard.

Finally, one additional point should be discussed regarding these cutoff-score-setting processes and related concepts. This has to do with the *use* of test scores. While these concepts and steps are useful for setting minimum standards, a criterion-related validity study may generate evidence that scores above minimum levels differentiate job performance. In such circumstances, using a cutoff score (or banding) may be justified, however, the level of adverse impact should also be considered.

Administering a PAT

Test administrators should be trained about the testing process prior to their being permitted to administer the test. Furthermore, it is recommended that if testing will take place over a lengthy period of time or uses multiple administrators, a lead administrator should be appointed to oversee the test's administration to ensure continuity between testing sessions. In addition, test administrators should faithfully follow the test event description plan that has been developed for the administration and scoring of each event. Deviating from the plan can result in increased potential liability to the employer.

Prior to the administration of each test event, candidates should be informed of the contents of that event. To help ensure standardization, which is fundamental for fair and valid testing, it is best if the administrator reads word-for-word from a script, or plays a recording, that describes each event before job candidates attempt those events. The administrator should also demonstrate (or show a video demonstrating) each event (including the different techniques that may be used for successfully performing the required task during each event).

In general, if a candidate appears to be confused or frustrated when taking the test, the administrator should ask, "Do you need me to repeat the instructions?" If the candidate answers yes, or if a candidate directly asks for additional instructions, the administrator should provide appropriate information. An exception to this would be if part of the testing criteria is the ability to follow the instructions of the test being administered. If that is the case, have a plan in place for how to address this issue in a job-related fashion (based on the job analysis and input from the job experts) in advance of testing.

Since many of the job candidates will be performing the events required during testing for the first time, it would make sense (in most situations) that they be given a longer amount of time, or allowed greater flexibility, to perform the task than if the task was being performed by someone who has been performing the job for a relatively long period of time. Similarly, the number of attempts to complete an event should be a realistic number that could be used to determine whether that job candidate could successfully perform a similar task on the job. In the interest of fairness, test takers should generally be allowed more than one attempt to complete an event, unless it is obvious that injury or harm would occur to the test taker (or others), and/or expensive or non-replaceable company property would be seriously damaged if another attempt was allowed. If testing is stopped because of the likelihood that injury or harm would occur if another attempt is allowed, this should be documented in detail and explained to the candidate.

In some instances, it might be acceptable to deduct points if instructions need to be provided to the test taker more than once during this type of test. However, deducting points or other penalties for this type of activity must be job related and justified in relationship to how the job is actually performed. For example, if there is no penalty on the job if an employee asks questions or clarifications when learning to perform a task, there should not be any penalty for this behavior during the test. Conversely, if the job requires that an employee learn a task and perform that task on the job without additional instructions, then taking this into consideration during testing may be justified.

When administering the PAT to candidates, the paramount concern should be the safety of each candidate. Safety can be promoted by ensuring that each candidate is shown the proper way(s) to perform each event prior to taking the test and by carefully observing the test takers during the events when appropriate.

Also, if relevant, the administrator should stress the importance of safety to the test taker before the test is administered. In addition, it might be helpful for someone to demonstrate how the test taker could safely use, maneuver, lift, carry, and/or move the materials during testing. To minimize potential injuries or problems during testing, it is strongly recommended that the test taker be allowed a reasonable period of time to practice lifting and/or carrying the materials/devices to be handled during each event. Administrators should also explain to the candidate that since safety is a primary concern, they will be disqualified if they do not follow the safety rules and/or safe work practices that have been explained to them. It might be helpful to provide a printed copy, in advance of administering the test, of any safety rules or safe work practices that will disqualify the job candidates if broken. Even if printed copies of the safety rules and safe work practices are given to the candidates in advance, those rules should be read, explained, and/or demonstrated to the candidates at the time of testing.[32] Employers should be aware that any actions they take during recruitment and testing sends a message to potential employees about the culture of the organization.

If a candidate violates a safety rule or if, during the physical ability or work-sample task event, they perform the task in a way that the administrator feels demonstrates that they do not possess the level of safety-related knowledge that a minimally-qualified, entry-level employee should possess, a complete and accurate description of that violation or unsafe work behavior should be presented to a panel of target-job experts (and/or supervisors and/or trainers of the target job) or safety committee members for evaluation.[33] Those experts shall determine whether the violation or unsafe work practice indicated that the candidate does not possess the level of safety-related knowledge or ability that a minimally-qualified, entry-level employee should possess. The job candidate will be disqualified if it is determined by the panel that his or her performance indicated he or she does not possess the level of safety-related knowledge or ability that a minimally-qualified, entry-level employee (for the target job) should possess prior to any training or on-the-job experience with the employer who is doing the testing.

Because the test will likely be physically strenuous, it is recommended that candidates be required to sign a waiver of liability (which must be completed and signed before a candidate is allowed to take the test). The liability release form should include a description of the test so that the candidate can make an informed decision to participate. If the employer so decides, candidates may also be required to obtain a medical release prior to testing. First aid and/or medical assistance should be readily available at the testing site.

If a candidate appears to be injured during testing, stop the test and ask him or her, "Are you injured?" If the candidate answers yes and/or it is obvious to the test administrator that he or she has injured him- or herself, stop the event and administer assistance immediately. In advance, plan how to respond to injuries that may occur during testing and make certain all test administrators are aware of the emergency response plan if an injury should occur.

The starting and ending points for each event, and/or the path that the test taker should take during testing, should be clearly marked for the test taker to see. For example, if the candidate can be penalized for traveling outside of a certain path during a test event, (1) the path limits should be clearly marked so the test taker knows his or her limits when performing a test event, and (2) the limits should be based upon solid, job-related reasons. For instance, there is a narrow path between two pieces of closely aligned equipment that must be followed when the job is actually performed, or a certain path must be carefully followed to avoid injuring an employee or another person on the job. It is helpful to photograph the test course to document that these steps have been taken.

In general, spectators should not be allowed during testing. However, even if there are no spectators, the candidates themselves will be observing each other perform the events. All observers and candidates should be instructed not to cheer, jeer, whistle, yell, signal, or in any way interfere with a fellow candidate's performance of an event. That being said, the test administrator is encouraged to provide a moderate, consistent level of encouragement, support, safety reminders, and/or instructions to all candidates.

If the testing requires strenuous physical activity, it is recommended that candidates be asked to remain at the testing site until they have sufficiently recovered from the testing process. This could potentially reduce claims and litigation related to testing. In general, candidates should not be permitted to leave the testing process until:

1. they have correctly performed the test events (administrators should make notes of any observable deficiencies);
2. the candidate says he or she wishes to stop the test or cannot complete the event (the candidate is then disqualified); or,
3. the candidate has attempted but did not successfully complete the event or test (the candidate is then disqualified).

Candidates who wish to leave prior to any of these three conditions should be asked, if possible, to sign a document indicating they have voluntarily withdrawn from the selection process. The administrator should carefully document the circumstances if the candidate refuses to sign such a document before leaving.

Scoring PATs

Scoring accuracy and fairness to all candidates can be promoted by implementing a standardized approach for the administration and scoring of each event (so that all candidates go through the same events, in the same sequence, and with the same instructions) and, if possible, utilizing multiple scorers (e.g., two individuals with stopwatches). Also, the same clear, unambiguous, observable criteria must be used when determining whether someone passes or fails the test event for each and every test taker. Ambiguous criteria, such as whether the test taker appeared to be struggling, was breathing hard, or had to stand on the tips of his or her toes when performing the task, are not acceptable for scoring purposes.

The final decision must be made as to whether the test taker successfully completed the task required or not, and within the defined observable criteria (such as being able to carry an object that weighs the same or less than the weight carried on the job; a job-related distance that is the same or less distance than on the job; or within a job-related amount of time that is the same or less than the amount of time in which the task must be performed on the job).

The amount of time a test taker uses to perform the test events should be measured carefully and recorded. To increase the reliability of time measurements, it is recommended that two administrators should time the test events whenever possible. The use of timers, where the candidate presses a button to begin the test event and presses the same button when he or she has completed the event, is also helpful.

Administrators should ensure that test results and information are recorded on the appropriate form(s). To minimize potential conflict later, it might be helpful if the scoring form is signed by both the test administrator and the job candidate at the end of testing. However, this is not generally required for a testing process to be considered valid.

The Americans with Disability Act (ADA) and PATs

As mentioned previously, testing that measures the test takers' physiological signs (such as heart or breathing rate) would be considered "medically-based" testing under the ADA. Medically-based tests can only be given after a bona fide offer of employment has been extended to the job candidate. Furthermore, the ADA specifies that applicants be required to perform the essential work functions with or without reasonable accommodations, that these be clearly described to applicants prior to job entry, and that they may be represented and measured on pre-employment tests. The EEOC indicates that "essential functions are the basic job duties that an employee must be able to perform, with or without reasonable accommodation."

Evidence of whether a particular function is essential includes, but is not limited to:

- the employer's judgment as to which function is essential;
- written job descriptions prepared before the advertising of, or interviewing of, applicants for a job;
- the amount of time spent on the job performing the function;

- the consequences of not requiring the incumbent to perform that function;

- the terms of a collective bargaining agreement;

- the work experience of past incumbents in the job; and/or,

- the current work experience of incumbents in similar jobs.[34]

While it may seem counterintuitive, an employer must provide reasonable accommodation to an applicant with a disability during testing even if that employer knows he or she will be unable to provide this individual with the same reasonable accommodation on the job because of undue hardship (which the employer must be prepared to prove). The EEOC warns employers to assess the need for accommodations for the application process separately from those that may be needed to perform the job.[35]

The next several sections provide data specific to the fire service industry but which are relevant and likely applicable to public safety industries in general. For example, the section below describes a physically-challenging test event that has been successfully used for determining whether firefighter candidates can perform that duty before they are hired. This illustrates the level of detail that is advised for developing and administering PATs within the public safety industry at large that would most likely survive a challenge.

Sample Test Event Description: Ladder Removal/Carry

Description: Candidate removes a twenty-four-foot aluminum extension ladder from mounted hooks, carries the ladder a minimum of sixty feet (around a diamond-shaped course, the boundaries of which are marked on the ground for applicants to follow), and replaces the ladder on to the same mounted hooks within three minutes.

Specifications:

- The twenty-four-foot aluminum extension ladder should weigh forty-one pounds.

- The mounted hooks should be positioned so that the top portion of the ladder is located forty-eight inches from the ground.

Demonstration to Candidates: Information that should be given to candidates during the demonstration:

There are three methods that may be used when completing this event: (1) the High-shoulder carry, (2) the Low-shoulder carry, and (3) the Suitcase carry. With all methods, candidates should begin by finding the balance point of the ladder. Rungs in the middle of the ladder, which should provide the best balance point, will be marked.

1. High-shoulder carry: In the high shoulder carry, the entire ladder sits on the top of the candidate's shoulder. Candidates may place the ladder directly on their shoulder from the mounted hooks and proceed around the designated area, replacing the ladder to the hooks directly from the shoulder.

2. Low-shoulder carry: In the low shoulder carry, the top beam of the ladder sits on the top of the candidate's shoulder. Candidates may place the ladder directly on their shoulder from the mounted hooks and proceed around the designated area, replacing the ladder to the hooks directly from the shoulder.

3. Suitcase carry: In this method, the top beam of the ladder is held in one arm like a suitcase.

If, in the administrator's opinion, the candidate loses control of the ladder while carrying it around the designated area, the administrator may intervene. The administrator will take the ladder from the candidate and place it on the ground at the place where the test taker lost control. The candidate can then pick the ladder up (in any fashion) and continue. When replacing the ladder, both ends of the ladder must be under the control of the test taker and off of the ground.

The ladder must be replaced on the hooks in the original position. There will be rungs marked on the ladder to assist candidates in this process. If the ladder is not replaced in the original position, candidates will be required to remove the ladder and replace it in the proper position.

Scoring:

While performing this event, candidates are allowed two penalties before failing. A penalty should be given if the:

- candidate drops the ladder, or if it touches the ground.
- candidate loses control of the ladder, and the administrator must step in and assist.
- candidate must place the ladder on the ground to gain stability.
- ladder falls over the neck of the candidate, with the candidate's neck between ladder rungs (in this case, the proctor should immediately assist in the removal and grounding of the ladder).
- candidate steps outside of the marked boundary path.
- candidate fails to follow instructions when performing the test event.
    - If the candidate fails to follow instructions when performing a test event, immediately stop the testing and timing of the event. Explain again how the event should be performed and, if appropriate, provide an additional demonstration. Ask the candidate to acknowledge that he

or she understands the instructions on how to properly perform the test event before allowing the candidate to continue, or start again, depending upon the circumstances. This should be allowed twice. If the candidate still does not follow the instructions after testing begins a third time, the candidate automatically fails this event and testing for that candidate should be discontinued.

Pass/Fail Criteria: The candidate will be automatically disqualified (fail) if a third penalty occurs or if the event is not successfully completed within three minutes.

Candidates should also be evaluated for their ability to work safely and/or follow safe working practices during the physical ability testing process. The administrator should carefully document if candidates:

- fail to follow the safety rules and/or procedures of which they had been made aware;

- ignore potential safety hazards that should have been obvious to a minimally-qualified, entry-level employee the first day on the job prior to training; or,

- perform in a way that is in violation of safety protocols that should have been obvious to a minimally-qualified, entry-level employee the first day on the job prior to training.

Methods Shown to Candidates:

- Safe lifting techniques (e.g., bend knees when lifting)
- Finding the balance point of the ladder
- Placing ladder directly on shoulder from mounted hooks
- High-shoulder carry
- Low-shoulder carry
- Suitcase carry
- Properly replacing the ladder (with both ends off of the ground and in the appropriate position)

Using PATs for Incumbents within Fire Safety

In 2000, the National Fire Protection Agency (NFPA) made a bold but profound statement: "Overweight, out-of-shape fire fighters are an accident waiting to happen" (2000). Research data shows that this statement really is true. For example, a 2005 study performed by the National Institute of Standards and Technology (NIST) revealed that nearly 50% of all injuries to civilian firefighters in that year were a result of sprains, strains, and muscular pain—whereby overexertion is considered the primary causative factor (2005).

Firefighters are charged with the serious responsibility of ensuring the safety of their crew and the public. Fire departments are motivated to reduce worker compensation claims, thereby reducing employment costs, which only constitutes some of the costs related to firefighter injuries. After tallying all of the costs related to firefighter injuries in 2002, NIST (2005) estimates the annual price to be between $2.8 and $7.8 billion.

This background shows why many fire department executives are passionate that their active fire suppression personnel have high fitness levels. While this may be the case, a national research survey of one hundred and eighty-five chief-level fire officers[36] revealed that only 25% of fire departments use PATs as annual maintenance standards for ensuring the fitness levels of their incumbent fire suppression personnel. This survey revealed that a much higher percentage (88%) use PATs for prescreening firefighters. So, while fire departments seem intent on screening fit candidates into their departments, maintenance-testing programs are not typically put into place to continually ensure the fitness level of incumbent fire personnel.

This is not because fire departments do not believe in the importance of ongoing testing. Indeed, this same survey revealed that 93% of the fire chiefs believed that "Active Fire Suppression Personnel should be tested annually to ensure that they possess the minimum physical abilities necessary to successfully perform the job." This shows overwhelming support for using PATs as a maintenance standard though only 25% of fire departments actually use PATs for maintenance purposes. This could be due to factors such as union influence and fear of employment lawsuits from personnel who cannot pass the PAT standard. The answers likely differ from department to department.

Regardless of the reasons why the majority (75%) of fire departments do not use a maintenance standard, the advantages of installing a PAT as a maintenance standard are worth serious consideration. In addition to the injuries, the costs from injuries, and the importance of protecting and preserving life and property, one must consider that firefighters age after they start the job, which has a direct impact on fitness levels. For example, one study[37] involving two hundred and fifty-six incumbent fire suppression personnel (with an average age of 34.83 years) revealed a very high correlation ($r = .397$) between age and test scores (in seconds) on a work-sample PAT. This correlation translates to roughly five seconds slower per year.

To put this into perspective, a twenty-five-year-old firefighter has a predicted score on the work-sample PAT of about eight minutes, whereas a fifty-year-old firefighter has a predicted score of ten minutes. This two-minute score difference is mostly attributable to age. This trend clearly indicates that aging, if left to its natural process without fitness-training interventions, will gradually move a minimally-qualified firefighter who (at age twenty-five) barely passed the job-related minimum cutoff score (nine minutes and thirty-four seconds on this particular PAT), to a score that is one full minute slower in just twelve years.

This phenomenon presents fire departments with the following options, to: (1) do nothing and cope with a workforce with naturally declining physical abilities; (2) institute a wellness program and hope that job-related standards associated with important fire suppression tasks are positively impacted; or, (3) institute a wellness program coupled with an annual maintenance standard using a work-sample PAT. The latter option works to ensure that active fire suppression personnel will maintain job performance standards.

Departments that adopt work-sample PATs as an annual maintenance standard must address three controversial issues: (1) selecting an appropriate cutoff time for the test as previously discussed (the same time used for entry-level or slower/faster), (2) choosing which positions will be selected for the annual testing requirement, and (3) identifying the steps that will be taken with incumbents who cannot pass the annual test even after repeated retest opportunities. These issues are addressed in the following section.

Which Positions Should Be Included in an Annual Maintenance Testing Program?

When fire chiefs who participated in the research study were asked the controversial question regarding which ranks should be required to pass an annual maintenance PAT, the results showed a clear cluster that included four ranks: Firefighter, Fire Engineer, Fire Lieutenant, and Fire Captain. Over 70% of the survey respondents were in clear agreement that maintenance PATs would be appropriately required for these positions. The next cluster included the Training Officer and Battalion Chief positions, which were both tied at about 60% agreement. The higher-level ranks (which included Fire Marshall, Division Chief, Assistant Chief, and Chief) fell between 30% and 40%, indicating that being able to pass an annual maintenance PAT was clearly less important for these ranks.

While the data in Figure 5-2 illustrates the findings from the fire service industry, it is likely that results would be similar had this survey been administered to police chiefs. Assuming that this is the case, implementing an annual incumbent maintenance test within the law enforcement industry would also be justified.

Figure 5-2. Fire Personnel Required to Pass Annual Maintenance PATs

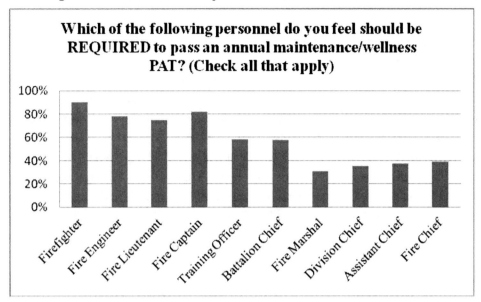

Figure 5-3 shows the percentage of time that various ranks spend in active fire suppression activities. These results reveal the reasons behind the results provided in Figure 5-2 (the importance of using a maintenance PAT is directly tied to the percentage of time that various ranks spend in fire suppression activities).

Figure 5-3. Percentage of Time Spent in Active Fire Suppression Activities (by rank)

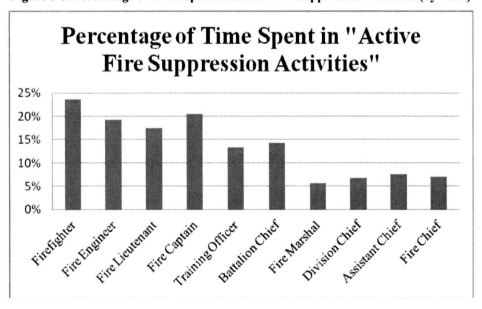

The study revealed that the average percentage of fire suppression calls was 21%, with a SD of 13.5%. The percentage of emergency medical service (EMS) calls was 71%, with a SD of 14.8%. There was no correlation between department size and type of calls, which reveals that the ratio of fire to EMS calls is not dependent on department size.

Choosing which positions to include in an annual maintenance-testing program should clearly be a department-by-department decision. With that said, the data reveal that the four positions that are traditionally hands-on when it comes to fire scene management should certainly be included in most situations. This includes the ranks of Firefighter, Fire Engineer, Fire Lieutenant, and Fire Captain. In most departments, the Training Officer is not directly involved in responding to fire emergencies. The Battalion Chief position, however, is different because field deployment levels of this position are sometimes high and will vary by assignment (e.g., training, administrative, etc.) as well as department size. The higher-level ranks (e.g., Fire Marshall, Division Chief, Assistant Chief, and Chief) will typically be exempt from maintenance programs.

What Steps Should Departments Take with Incumbents Who Fail Annual Maintenance Standards?

The research conducted on this issue included a question that asked respondents: "Which of the following consequences do you feel are acceptable for ACTIVE FIRE SUPPRESSION incumbents who cannot pass a maintenance/wellness PAT?" The four response options that were provided to respondents were:

- Conditioning program—the incumbent is placed on a program that includes dietary modification and physical training.

- Leave of absence—the department may elect to place the incumbent on a leave of absence until which time the incumbent is able to pass the test.

- Disability leave—the department may elect to place the incumbent on disability leave until the incumbent is able to pass the test.

- Retirement with pension—the department may elect to terminate employment with the incumbent following continued attempts to improve test performance without success.

The results from this survey question are provided in Figure 5-4.

Figure 5-4. Consequences for Failing Maintenance PATs

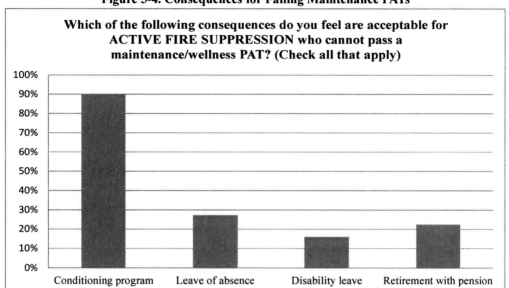

Which of the following consequences do you feel are acceptable for
ACTIVE FIRE SUPPRESSION who cannot pass a
maintenance/wellness PAT? (Check all that apply)

Figure 5-4 shows that most responding chiefs (90%) agreed that requiring a
conditioning program was a logical natural consequence for incumbents who cannot
pass a maintenance PAT. However, a significant portion of the chiefs stated that more
severe consequences (taking a leave of absence or retirement with pension) would also
be justified (with 27% and 22% endorsement, respectively). Only 15% endorsed the
most extreme consequence of required disability leave.

Before moving to one of these three severe consequences, we suggest first
allowing the candidate (up to) two retesting opportunities (each separated by a ten-to-
sixteen-week training program). The ten-to-sixteen-week training program should
consist of both cardiovascular and strength training in the specific fire suppression-
related work behaviors that are measured by the test. Departments can choose whether
they want the training program to be self-directed or conducted by a department-
designated exercise specialist.

Age and Gender Norming within the Public Safety Industry

There is a growing concern that the age and gender of the incumbent will affect
performance on the PAT and that adjustments should be made to address these factors.
However, Section 106 of the 1991 CRA prohibits the use of gender-based standards,
stating:

> It shall be unlawful employment practice for a respondent, in
> connection with the selection or referral of applicants or candidates for
> employment or promotion, to adjust the scores of, use different cutoff

scores for, or otherwise alter the results of, employment related tests on the basis of race, color, religion, sex or national origin.

Additionally, the ADA of 1990 states that employee standards must be job related. Specifically, Section 103 of the ADA states:

(a) In general. - It may be a defense to a charge of discrimination under this that an alleged application of qualification standards, tests, or selection criteria that screen out or tend to screen out or otherwise deny a job or benefit to an individual with a disability has been shown to be job-related and consistent with business necessity, and such performance cannot be accomplished by reasonable accommodation, as required under this subchapter.

(b) Qualification standards. - The term "qualification standards" may include a requirement that an individual shall not pose a direct threat to the health or safety of other individuals in the workplace.

Given the nature of jobs within the public safety industry and the consequence of error associated with an applicant or incumbent who is unable to perform the critical duties, adjusting a PAT cutoff score based on age or gender, for either applicants or incumbents, not only violates the CRA of 1991 and the ADA of 1990, but could very likely put the health and safety of personnel and the public in danger.

Chapter 6—Building a Balanced Hiring Program

The best testing process for screening entry-level applicants is one that consists of using the wide range of tests, previously discussed, to measure a wide range of abilities specific to the position. It will also necessarily be an arduous process; by the time each applicant's resume, background, written, and interview results have been reviewed, tallied, and scored, the time investment typically exceeds several hours per candidate; however, the rewards of using such a process more than offset the effort involved.

The first step in building a balanced hiring program is to choose which tests to use and which competency areas to measure. According to the results of a national survey (see Table 6-1) that was completed by one hundred and thirty fire executives (fire chiefs of all levels) and eighty-one law enforcement executives (law enforcement officers of all levels), the three most important competency areas needed for their field's entry-level position are:[38]

- cognitive/academic (such as reading, math, and writing);

- personal characteristics (such as working under stress, allegiance, and integrity); and,

- physical abilities (such as upper body strength, stamina, and speed).

A similar survey was conducted among law enforcement officers, which ranked the order of importance in two major competency areas (see Table 6-2):

- cognitive/academic (spelling/punctuation and writing ability); and,

- personal characteristics (such as self-control, interpersonal skills, and ability to enforce laws).

The surveys revealed that supervisory personnel valued the cognitive/academic domains for both entry-level positions. It should be pointed out that most professionals who have seasoned their careers in public safety would be the first to admit that the typical entry-level testing process does not reflect these ratios. In fact, most testing processes focus on the cognitive/academic areas (typically through a pass/fail written test), use a basic PAT (again, pass/fail), and only measure a very limited degree of personal characteristics through an interview process (but only for the final few candidates who are competing for a small number of open positions).

Table 6-1. Entry-Level Firefighter Competency Weights

Cognitive/Academic (32% of Total)	% of Importance
Math	10%
Reading	14%
Verbal Communication	15%
Writing	12%
Map Reading	8%
Problem Solving	15%
Strategic Decision-Making	13%
Mechanical Ability	12%
Personal Characteristics (40% of Total)	**% of Importance**
Teamwork	12%
Working under Stress	10%
Allegiance/Loyalty	9%
Truthfulness/Integrity	13%
Public Relations	8%
Emotional Stability	10%
Sensitivity	8%
Proactive/Goal-Oriented	8%
Thoroughness/Attention to Detail	9%
Following Orders	10%
Physical Abilities (28% of Total)	**% of Importance**
Wrist/Forearm Strength	13%
Upper Body Strength	17%
Lower Torso and Leg Strength	17%
Speed	12%
Dexterity, Balance, and Coordination	16%
Endurance	21%

Table 6-2. Entry-Level Law Enforcement Officer Competency Weights

Cognitive/Academic (39% of Total)	% of Importance
Spelling/Punctuation	38%
Writing Ability	62%
Personal Characteristics (61% of Total)	**% of Importance**
Integrity	17%
Decision-Making	13%
Law Enforcement Code of Ethics	12%
Interpersonal Skills	9%
Stress Tolerance	7%
Self-Control	6%
Teamwork	6%
Acceptance	5%
Confidentiality	5%
Enforcement of Laws	5%
Following Orders	5%
Respect	5%
Self-Discipline	5%

Not only does this result in a disconnect between the competencies that are required for the job and those that are included in the screening process, it also results in hiring processes that can unnecessarily cause adverse impact on minorities and/or women. For example, a hiring process that focuses exclusively on cognitive/academic skills will magnify adverse impact against minorities because the subject matter of standardized testing material has been known to be less accessible to minority groups. A hiring process that overemphasizes the importance of physical abilities will amplify adverse impact against women. The other cost for using an unbalanced hiring process is that it produces a massive vacuum (40%, to be precise) in the personal characteristics area, leaving these important competencies completely unmeasured.

Beyond the adverse impact issues, other substantial problems occur when a fire department adopts an unbalanced hiring process. A testing process that does not adequately measure important cognitive/academic criteria will likely result in the acquisition of cadets who lack intellectual capabilities, which can lead to poor on-the-job performance. On the other hand, over-measuring this area while under-measuring personal characteristics, could lead to a group of book-smart firefighters who have no idea how to work cooperatively in the close living conditions required of their position. Under-measuring physical abilities in the hiring process while over-measuring personal characteristics could result in a group of firefighters who cannot perform the strenuous physical requirements of the job, especially as they age. Clearly, it is important in the testing process to find a balanced approach.

Challenges and Recommendations for Success

The most significant challenge to building effective testing programs for entry-level firefighters and police officers lies with testing interpersonal skills (personal characteristics). This is because these skills—such as teamwork and interpersonal skills—are crucial ingredients for success, but they are the most difficult to measure in a typical testing format. For example, developing a math test is easy while developing a test for measuring teamwork skills is not, though the latter was rated as more important for overall job success in both the entry-level firefighter and entry-level law enforcement officer positions.

The reason for this is that many skills and abilities are concrete (as opposed to being theoretical and abstract). An applicant's math skills can be readily tapped using questions that measure numerical skills at the same level that is required on the job. Abstract or soft skills like teamwork are more difficult to measure during a one- or two-hour testing session.

Fortunately, there are some effective and innovative testing solutions available. Tables 6-3 through 6-7 on the following pages provide suggested test methodologies and tools for each of the key competencies needed for being a well-rounded firefighter or law enforcement officer.

**Table 6-3. Proposed Solutions for Testing Cognitive/Academic Competencies
of Entry-Level Firefighters**

C/A (32% Overall Importance)	Weight	Proposed Testing Solution	Typical Validation Method
Math	10%	Use written or "work-sample" format; measure using a limited number of multiple-choice items. Balance various types of math skills (add/subtract/multiply/divide, etc.).	CV
Reading	14%	Measure using either (1) *Test Preparation Manual* approach (where the applicants are given a manual and asked to study it for a few weeks prior to taking the test based on the manual; or (2) a short reading passage containing material at a similar difficulty/context to the job that applicants are allowed to study during the testing session and use to answer related test items.	CV
Verbal Communication	15%	While a structured interview is the best tool for measuring this skill (because the skill includes verbal and nonverbal aspects), some level of this skill can be measured using word recognition lists or sentence clarity items.	CV
Writing	12%	Measure using writing passages or word recognition lists, sentence clarity, and/or grammar evaluation items.	CV
Map Reading	8%	Measure using maps and related questions asking applicants how they would maneuver to certain locations. Include directional awareness.	CV
Problem Solving	15%	Measure using word problems that measure reasoning skills in job-rich contexts.	CRV
Strategic Decision-Making	13%	While a structured interview is the best tool for measuring this skill (because the applicant can be asked to apply this skill in firefighter-specific scenarios), some level of this skill can be measured using word problems or other contexts supplied in written format where applicants can consider cause/effect of certain actions.	CV
Mechanical Ability	12%	Using CV, measure mechanical comprehension skills such as leverage, force, and mechanical/physics contexts regarding weights, shapes, and distances. Can also measure spatial reasoning (when using a CRV validation strategy).	CV/CRV

Note: C/A: Cognitive/Academic; CV: Content Validity; and CRV: Criterion-related validity

**Table 6-4. Proposed Solutions for Testing Personal Characteristics
of Entry-Level Firefighters**

Personal Characteristics (40% Overall)	Weight	Proposed Testing Solution	Typical Validation Method
Teamwork	12%	Under a CV strategy, a Situational Judgment Test (SJT) can be used for measuring these skills. Alternatively, a custom personality test can be developed using CRV. While these types of assessments can measure whether an applicant knows the most appropriate response (using an SJT) or has the best attitude or disposition (personality test), they are limited in that they cannot measure whether an applicant would actually respond in such a way. For these reasons, measuring the underlying traits that tend to generate these positive behaviors is typically the most effective strategy. Structured interviews can also provide useful insight into these types of competencies, as well as background and reference evaluations. However, these tools are time consuming and expensive, so measuring these areas in the testing stage is an effective strategy.	CV/CRV
Working under Stress	10%		
Allegiance/Loyalty	9%		
Truthfulness/Integrity	13%		
Public Relations	8%		
Emotional Stability	10%		
Sensitivity	8%		
Proactive/Goal-Oriented	8%	These competencies can be effectively measured using either a SJT (using a CV or CRV strategy) or a Conscientiousness (CS) scale (using a CRV strategy). A CS test can be developed using just 20-30 items (using Likert-type responses). Such tests are typically successful in predicting job performance in fire settings.	CV/CRV
Thoroughness/ Attention to Detail	9%		
Following Orders	10%		

Note: CV: Content Validity; and CRV: Criterion-related validity.

Table 6-5. Proposed Solutions for Testing Physical Abilities of Entry-Level Firefighters

Physical Abilities (28% Overall)	Weight	Proposed Testing Solution	Typical Validation Method
Wrist/Forearm Strength	13%	It is the opinion of the authors that these unique physical competencies should be collectively and representatively measured in a work-sample style PAT (using a content validity strategy). While other types of tests (such as clinical strength tests) that do not directly mirror the requirements of the job can be used (if they are based on CRV), using a high-fidelity work sample typically has greater benefits.	CV
Upper Body Strength	17%		CV
Lower Torso/Leg Strength	17%		CV
Dexterity, Balance, Coordination	16%		CV
Speed	12%	Strenuous work-sample PATs can measure some level of endurance (and speed) if they are continuously-timed and exceed at least five minutes in length. Actual cardiovascular endurance levels can only be measured using a post-job-offer V02 maximum test (which would require using a CRV strategy).	CV/CRV

Note: CV: Content Validity; and CRV: Criterion-related validity.

Tables 6-6 and 6-7 provide suggested test methodologies and tools for each of the key competencies needed for being a fully rounded law enforcement officer.

Table 6-6. Proposed Solutions for Testing Cognitive/Academic Competency for Entry-Level Law Enforcement Officers

Personal Characteristics (39% Overall)	Weight	Proposed Testing Solution	Typical Validation Method
Spelling/ Punctuation	32%	The ability to use correct spelling and punctuation in writing sufficient to: (a) convert information given orally into written form; (b) prepare written narrative and statistical reports, letters, memoranda, and forms in accordance with department procedures; (c) write traffic citations; and (d) enter computer data.	CV
Writing Ability	68%	The ability to write clearly, accurately, concisely, legibly, and with correct English. Grammatical construction sufficient to: (a) convert information given orally to written form; (b) prepare written narrative and statistical reports, letters, memoranda, and forms in accordance with department procedures; (c) write traffic citations; and (d) enter computer data.	CV

Note: CV: Content Validity.

Table 6-7. Proposed Solutions for Testing Personal Characteristics for Entry-Level Law Enforcement Officers

Personal Characteristics (61% Overall)	Weight	Proposed Testing Solution	Typical Validation Method
Integrity	17%	Under a CV strategy, a Situational Judgment Test (SJT) can be used for measuring these skills. Alternatively, a custom personality test can be developed using CRV. While these types of assessments can measure whether an applicant knows the most appropriate response (using a SJT) or has the best attitude or disposition (personality test), they are limited in that they cannot measure whether an applicant would actually respond in such a way. For these reasons, measuring the underlying traits that tend to generate these positive behaviors is typically the most effective strategy. Structured interviews can also provide useful insight into these types of competencies, as well as background and reference evaluations. However, these tools are time consuming and expensive, so measuring these areas in the testing stage is an effective strategy.	CV/CRV
Decision-Making	13%		
Law Enforcement Code of Ethics	12%		
Interpersonal Skills	9%		
Stress Tolerance	7%		
Self-Control	6%		
Teamwork	6%		
Acceptance	5%		
Confidentiality	5%		
Enforcement of Laws	5%		
Following Orders	5%	These competencies can be effectively measured using either a SJT (using a CV or CRV strategy) or a Conscientiousness (CS) scale (using a CRV strategy). A CS test can be developed using just 20–30 items (using Likert-type responses). Such tests are typically successful in predicting job performance in fire settings.	CV/CRV
Respect	5%		
Self-Discipline	5%		

Note: CV: Content Validity; and CRV: Criterion-related validity.

The importance weights displayed in the tables above may or may not be representative of individual fire departments and law enforcement agencies. For example, some fire departments serve communities that have more multiple structure or high-rise fires than others, some have a higher occurrence rate of EMS incidents, and so on. Therefore, we recommend that each department investigate the relative importance of these various competencies and the tests used to measure them (discussed further in the next section).

Developing, Validating, and Analyzing Written Tests

Written Test Development Steps

Step 1: Determine the KSAPCs to Be Measured by the Test

The selection plan can be used for selecting the KSAPCs that can be measured by the written test (see Chapter 3). If a selection plan has not been completed, consider using the criteria below as baselines. The KSAPCs selected for the written test should be:

1. needed on the first day of the job;

2. important or critical (necessary) for the performance of the job;[39]

3. linked to one or more critical (necessary) job duties; and,

4. for job knowledge only, rated sufficiently high on the Level Needed for Success rating (see the Job Analysis Section in Chapter 3). This is necessary for insuring that the job-knowledge domains measured by the test are needed (on the first day of hire) at a level that requires the applicant to have the information already in memory (written tests should not measure aspects of a job knowledge that can simply be looked up or referenced by incumbents on the job without seriously impacting job performance).

It is important to note that the KSAPCs selected for measurement on the written test should meet these criteria both generally (as defined in the job analysis) and specifically (each of the separate facets or aspects of the selected KSAPCs should also meet these criteria). For example, if basic math is required for a job and it meets the criteria above, test items should not be developed for measuring advanced math skills.

Step 2: Develop a Test Plan for Measuring the Selected KSAPCs

The three areas that should be addressed for developing a solid written test plan are:

1. the general components of a test plan;

2. the number of test items; and,

3. the types of test items.

General Components of a Test Plan

The elements and steps necessary for a written test plan will vary based on the types of KSAPCs measured by the test. The components below should therefore be regarded as general requirements:

- What is the purpose of the test? Will it be used to qualify only those who possess mastery levels of the KSAPC? Advanced levels? Baseline levels?

- Will the test be scored in a multiple hurdle or compensatory fashion? Multiple-hurdle tests require applicants to obtain a passing score on each section of the written test. Compensatory tests allow an applicant's high score in one area to compensate for an area in which he or she scored low. A multiple-hurdle strategy should be used if certain baseline levels of proficiency are required for each KSAPC measured by the test while a compensatory approach can be used if the developer will allow higher levels of one KSAPC to compensate for lower levels of another, on the test. Evaluating how the KSAPCs are required and used on the job is a key consideration for making this decision.

- What is the target population being tested? Has the applicant population been pre-screened using minimum qualification requirements?

- Will the test be a speeded test or a power test? A test is categorized as a speeded test when time is considered an element of measurement on the test (for reasons that are related to the job) and it can be used to differentiate between candidates (some tests based on criterion-related validity are designed with speed as an essential component of the test). With a power test, at least 95% of the applicants are usually able to complete the test within the allotted time. Most written tests are administered as power tests.

- What reading level will be used for the test? Most word processing programs include features for checking the grade reading level of the test, which should be slightly below the reading level required at entry to the job.

- What will the delivery mode be for the test (e.g., paper/pencil, oral, computer-based)?

- What scoring processes and procedures will be used?

- Will a test preparation or study guide be provided to applicants? Test preparation and study guides can be developed at many levels, ranging from a cursory overview of the test and its contents to an explicit description of the KSAPCs that will be measured.

- Will test preparation sessions be offered to the applicants?

Choosing the Number of Test Items

Some of the key considerations regarding selecting the number of items to include on the written test are:

- Make an adequate sampling of the KSAPC measured. A sufficient number of items should be developed to effectively measure each KSAPC at the desired level. Note that some KSAPCs will require more items than others for making a sufficiently deep assessment of the levels held by the applicants. Be sure that the important aspects of each KSAPC are included in the test plan.

- Make a proportional sampling of the KSAPCs. This pertains to the number of items measuring each KSAPC compared with others. The test should be internally weighted in a way that ensures a robust measurement of the relevant KSAPCs (this is discussed in detail below). Special consideration should be given to this proportional sampling requirement when developing job-knowledge tests.

- Include a sufficient number of items to generate high test reliability. While there are numerous factors that impact test reliability, perhaps the single most important factor is the overall number of test items per relevant KSAPC in the test.

There are no hard-and-fast rules regarding the number of items to include for measuring a KSAPC. A developer can have a few or many test items for any testable KSAPC (those that meet the criteria above); however, some rational or empirical process for internally weighting the written test is helpful and usually makes the test more effective. Here are some guidelines to consider:

- Some KSAPCs are more complex or broad than others and thus may require more test items for adequate measurement. For example, finding out how much an applicant knows about advanced physics may require more items than would be adequate for assessing his or her simple multiplication skills.

- If several discrete KSAPCs will be measured on the same written test, be sure that they are not divergent. If they are, put them on separate tests (or on the same test as a subscale that is scored separately).[40] If the test will be scored and used as one overall assessment with one final score for each applicant, the various KSAPCs on the test will need to be homogeneous (so they have similar types of variance because they are based on similar or inter-related content and items of similar difficulty levels). If one KSAPC is substantially different from others on the same test, the test items can work against each other and decrease the overall test reliability (making the interpretation of a single score for the test inaccurate).

- As a general rule, do not measure a discrete KSAPC with fewer than twenty items, and be sure that the overall test includes at least sixty items if measuring more than one KSAPC. This will help ensure that the test will have sufficiently high reliability.

One of the factors for choosing the number of items (and for which KSAPC) to include on a test is to internally weight the test in a way that is relevant to the requirements of the job. One effective system for developing internal weights is to have job experts assign point values to the various sections of the test (as previously exemplified when job experts were asked to assign one hundred points among the main KSAPCs for firefighters).

The drawback to using this approach is that the items will now require polytomous weighting (e.g., 0.8 points for the items measuring Skill A, 1.2 points for each item measuring Skill B, etc.). This can be avoided by allotting the same number of points to each item (i.e., each item in each section of the test is worth one point) and then adding (or removing) items to each section so that the point total matches the weights provided by job experts. During this process, it is important to avoid having too few items in any given section.

Choosing the Type of Test Items

What type of test items should be included on the test to measure the KSAPCs—complex? easy? difficult? When measuring job-knowledge domains, should items that measure the difficult, complex, and evaluative aspects of knowledge be included? Or should items that only cover the simple facts and definitions be included? The key consideration regarding selecting the type of items for a test is to make sure that the KSAPCs are measured in a relevant way using items that are appropriately geared to the level of the KSAPC that is required on the job.

One helpful tool for making item type decisions is using Bloom's Taxonomy (Bloom, 1956), which can be adopted as a model for developing written test items that measure the intended KSAPC at various levels. See Table 6-8 for an illustration of Bloom's Taxonomy for Item Writing.

Table 6-8. Bloom's Taxonomy for Item Writing

Level	Skill Demonstrated	Test Item Stem
	Bloom's Taxonomy for Item Writing	
	Skill Demonstrated	Test Item Stem
1 - Knowledge	Recall factual information	List the three major …
	Knowledge of dates, events, places	Define the four parts of …
	Terminology	What is the definition of …?
	Basic knowledge of major ideas	Which author …?
	Major classifications and categories	Who was responsible for …?
2 - Comprehension	Grasp key meanings	What is the difference between …?
	Apply knowledge to a different context	Which of the following would occur …?
	Infer causation	Summarize the major …
	Compare/contrast	Use the following to estimate…
	Determine sequences	How are these two similar …?
3 - Application	Use information to solve problems	Apply the concept of X to solve for Y …
	Apply methods, theories, or calculations	What are the steps for completing …?
	Diagnose the possible outcomes	Calculate the X of Y …
	Reduce to most plausible best answer	Complete the following by using …
	Analyze within a concrete framework	Which of the following best describes …?
4 - Analysis	Detect patterns	Analyze and determine …
	Comprehend in-depth meanings	Which of the following would not …?
	Evaluate organization of multiple parts	What are the key differences between …?
	Break down complex system into parts	Explain the difference between…
	Diagnose complete systems	What are the key similarities between …?
5 - Synthesis	Make abstractions	Which of the following would occur …?
	Make generalizations from a set of facts	What would be the necessary steps to …?
	Make likely predictions	What would need to be substituted …?
	Draw conclusions based on ideas	Order the following by importance …
	Make logical inferences	How could X be rebuilt if Y …?
6 - Evaluation	Discriminate between theories or ideas	Which of the following is the best …?
	Argue to a conclusion	Rank order the proposed solutions …
	Detect biases or faulty conclusions	Which of the following would …?
	Make critical judgments using inferences	Assess and select the best …
	Diagnose the most effective solutions	What would likely happen if …?

Test developers can use this taxonomy (or an abbreviated version) to provide guidance for developing items that are at an appropriate level for the job (considering how the KSAPC is applied on the job—e.g., factual recall, application, analysis, etc.).

Another factor to consider regarding the item type is the format of the item. Common formats include multiple choice, true/false, open-ended, or essay. Multiple choice is perhaps the most common format used for fixed-response items (items with only a limited number of alternative options)—and for a good reason. Applicants have a 50% likelihood of guessing the correct answer for true/false items and only 25% likelihood for multiple choice items with four alternatives (or 20% likelihood for items with five alternatives).

Open-ended and essay formats require subjective scoring, which can be time consuming and costly. Another drawback with subjective scoring is that another type of unreliability enters into the equation when the tests are scored: inter-rater reliability. Inter-rater reliability relates to the consistency between scorers who subjectively grade the tests. While there is nothing wrong with these types of item formats (in fact they are the best item formats to use to test for the higher level of Bloom's Taxonomy), they will not be discussed further in this text for the reasons stated above.

Step 3: Develop the Test Content

Test items can be developed by personnel professionals and/or job experts. If job experts are used, begin at step 1; if experienced test developers are used, begin at step 5:

1. Select a panel of four to ten job experts who are truly experts in the content area and are diverse in terms of ethnicity, gender, geography, seniority (use a minimum of one year of experience), and functional areas of the target position. Supervisors and trainers can also be included.

2. Review the selection plan, test plan, and validation surveys (discussed below) that will be used to validate the test. This step is critical because the job experts should be very well informed regarding the KSAPCs measured by the test (and their affiliated job duties) and the number and types of items to be included on the test.

3. Have each job expert review and sign a confidentiality agreement. In addition, create an atmosphere of confidentiality and request that no documents or notes be taken out of the workshop room. Lock the doors when taking breaks.

4. Conduct a training session on item writing (various guidelines are available for this online). The training should conclude with an opportunity for job experts to write sample test items and then exchange and critique the items using the techniques learned in the training.

5. Write test items following the selection plan and test plan. Be sure that item writers reference the validation survey that will be used by the validation panel so that the items will address the criteria used by this panel for validating the items. When determining the number of items to write according to the test plan, double the number of items that are slated for measuring each KSAPC. This is necessary because the validation process will eliminate some of the items. Excess items can also be used to replace items that show poor item statistics. A Test Item Form should be used by item writers to record the KSAPCs measured, correct answer, textual reference including distractor references (for job-knowledge items), and other useful information for each draft item.

6. Have the item writers exchange and critique items, paying careful attention to:

    a. grammar, style, and consistency;

    b. selection plan and test plan requirements; and,

    c. criteria on the validation survey.

(Do not be afraid to delete a poor item early in the development/validation process. Keep only the best items at this phase in the process.)

7. Create a final version of the draft test that is ready for review by the validation panel. This version of the test should include the item, KSAPC measured, correct answer, and textual reference with distractor references (for job-knowledge items).

Step 4: Validate the Test

Validating a written test requires convening a group of qualified job experts and having them review and rate the written test using several factors. Some of these factors include the quality of the test items, fairness, relationship to the job, and proficiency level required. A suggested list of rating questions that can be used is provided below:

1. Regarding the quality of the test item, does it:

    a. read well? Is it clear and understandable?

    b. provide sufficient information to answer correctly?

    c. contain distractors that are similar in difficulty? distinct? incorrect yet plausible? similar in length? correctly matching the stem?

    d. have an answer key that is correct in all circumstances?[41]

    e. provide clues to other items on the test?

    f. ask the question in a way that is free from unnecessary complexities?

    g. ask the question in a way that is fair to all groups?

2. Regarding the job-relatedness of the item, does it:

    a. link to an important or critical KSAPC that is needed the first day of the job?

    b. link to an important or critical job duty (job experts should identify this using job duty numbers from the job analysis)? (Note: if the KSAPCs measured by the test have already been linked to essential job duties, this step is not required, but can be helpful.)

3. Regarding the proficiency level required for the KSAPC measured by the item, what percent of minimally-qualified applicants would job experts expect to answer this item correctly? (This data can be used for setting validated cutoff scores.)

4. For job-knowledge tests:

    a. Is the item based on current information?

    b. Does it measure an aspect of job knowledge that must be memorized?

    c. How serious are the consequences if the applicant does not possess the knowledge required to answer this item correctly?

Validation Criteria for Test Items

There are no firm minimum criteria that specifically apply to any of the key validation factors offered in the Uniform Guidelines or in the professional standards. In fact, it is quite possible to have a written test that could be considered as an overall valid selection procedure, but that includes several items that would be rated negatively on the ratings proposed above. However, the goal is to have every item address these criteria.

There are a few seminal court cases that can provide guidance on some of these key validation criteria. Two of these high-level court cases are *Contreras v. City of Los Angeles* (1981) and *United States v. South Carolina* (1978). Because of the transportable concepts regarding written test validation that have been argued and decided in these cases, they have also been frequently referenced in other cases involving written tests. Because the judges in each of these cases ultimately supported the development and validation work surrounding the tests involved, they are worth discussing here.

In *Contreras*, a three-phase process was used to develop and validate an examination for an auditor position. In the final validation phase, where the job experts were asked to identify a knowledge, skill, or ability that was measured by the test item, a "5 out of 7" rule (71%) was used to screen items for inclusion on the final test. After extensive litigation, the Ninth Circuit approved the validation process of constructing a written test using this process.

In *South Carolina*, job experts were convened into ten-member panels and asked to provide certain judgments to evaluate whether each item on the tests (which included nineteen subtests on a National Teacher Exam used in the state) involved subject matter that was a part of the curriculum at the teacher-training institution and was appropriate for testing. These review panels determined that between 63% and 98% of the items on the various tests were content valid and relevant for use in South Carolina. The US Supreme Court endorsed this process as "sufficiently valid."

These two cases provide useful guidance for establishing the minimum thresholds (71% and 63%, respectively) of job expert endorsement necessary (for on-the-job-relatedness questions) for screening test items and including them on a final test. It is important to note that, in both of these cases, at least an "obvious majority" of the job experts was required to justify that the items were sufficiently related to the job to be selected for the final test.

Step 5: Score and Analyze the Test

An important part of analyzing the test is breaking down the theoretical into something that the average practitioner can actually use in everyday work. This section aims to achieve this goal. While there is no escaping that test analysis requires the use of advanced statistical tools, some of these can be automated by software. Many of them can even be completed in common spreadsheet programs. The purpose of this section is to equip the reader with a basic knowledge regarding some of the fundamental, essential components of test analysis and (most importantly) interpretation rules that can be applied to look for problem areas.

Classical test analyses[42] (conducted after a test has been administered) can be broken down into two primary categories: item-level analyses and test-level analyses. Item-level analyses investigate the statistical properties of each item as they relate to other items and to the overall test. Test-level analyses focus on how the test is working at an overall level. The item-level analyses will be reviewed first.

Item-Level Analyses

While there are numerous item-analysis techniques available, only three of the most essential are reviewed here: item-test correlations (called "point biserial" correlations), item difficulty, and DIF. Item discrimination indices are also useful for conducting item-level analyses, but are not discussed in this text.

Point Biserials

Point biserial calculations result in values between -1.0 and +1.0 that reveal the correlation between the item and the overall test score. Items that have negative values are typically either poor items (with respect to what they are measuring, how they are worded, or both) or are good items that are simply entered incorrectly. Values between 0.0 and +0.2 indicate that the item is functioning somewhat effectively but is not contributing to the overall reliability of the test in a meaningful way. Values of +0.2 and higher indicate that the item is functioning in an effective way and is contributing to the overall reliability of the test. For this reason, the single best way to increase the reliability of the overall test is to remove items with low (or negative) point biserials.

The point biserial of a test item can be calculated by simply correlating the applicant's score on the test item (coded 0 for incorrect, 1 for correct) to their total score on the overall test using the Pearson formula in Microsoft Excel, as previously mentioned. When the total number of items on the test is fewer than thirty, a corrected version of this calculation can be run by removing the score of each item from the total score calculation (e.g., when calculating a point biserial for item 1, correlate item 1 to the total score on the test using items 2–30; for item 2, include only items 1 and 3–30 for the total score).

Item Difficulty

Item difficulties show the percentage of applicants who answered the item correctly. Items that are excessively difficult or easy (where a very high proportion of test takers are either missing the item or answering it correctly) are typically the items that do not contribute significantly to the overall reliability of the test and should be considered for removal. Typically, items that provide the highest contribution to the overall reliability of the test are in the midrange of difficulty (e.g., 40% to 60%).

Differential Item Functioning (DIF)

DIF analyses detect items that are not functioning in similar ways between the focal and reference groups. The Standards explain that DIF "occurs when different groups of applicants with similar overall ability, or similar status on an appropriate criterion, have, on average, systematically different responses to a particular item." In some instances, DIF analyses can reveal items that are biased against certain groups (test bias can be defined as any quality of the test item, or the test, that offends or unnecessarily penalizes some applicants on the basis of personal characteristics such as ethnicity, gender, etc.).

It should be noted that there is a very significant difference between simply reviewing the average item score differences between groups (e.g., men and women) and DIF analyses. One might be tempted to simply evaluate the proportion of men who answered the item correctly (say 80%) versus the proportion of women (say 60%) and then note the size of the difference (20%) when compared to other items on the test with more or less spread between groups.

The major flaw with this approach is that it fails to take group ability levels into account. What if men simply have a 20% higher ability level than women on the KSAPC measured by the test? Does this make the test, or the items with this level of difference, unfair or biased? Certainly not. In fact, this simple difference approach was used in one court case, but received an outcry of disagreement from the professional testing community.

The case was *Golden Rule Life Insurance Company v. Mathias* (1980) and involved the Educational Testing Service (ETS) and the Illinois Insurance Licensure Examination. In a consent decree related to this case, the parties agreed that test items could be divided into categories (and some items removed) based only on the average item score differences on individual items. This practice did not consider or statistically control for the overall ability differences between groups on the test and was subsequently abandoned after the president of ETS renounced the practice, stating:

> the practice was a mistake ... [and] it has been used to justify legislative proposals that go far beyond the very limited terms of the original agreement.... We recognized that the settlement compromise was not based on an appropriate "bias prevention" methodology for tests generally. What was to become known as the "Golden Rule" procedure is based on the premise—which ETS did not and does not share—that group differences in performance on test questions primarily are caused by "bias." The procedure ignores the possibility that differences in performance may validly reflect real differences in knowledge or skill. (Anrig, 1987)

The criteria used in the *Golden Rule* case also sparked dissent in the professional testing community:

> The final settlement of the case was based on a comparison of group differences in sheer percentage of persons passing an item, with no effort to equate groups in any measure of the ability the test was designed to assess, nor any consideration of the validity of items for the intended purpose of the test. The decision was clearly in complete violation of the concept of differential item functioning and would be likely to eliminate the very items that were the best predictors of job performance. (Anastasi, 1997)

So, it is safe to say that the professional testing community sufficiently rebuked the idea of simply comparing group differences on items or tests overall. This is precisely where DIF analyses provide a significant contribution to test analyses. Because DIF analyses are different than simple average item score differences between groups and take overall group ability into consideration when detecting potentially biased items, some courts have specifically approved the use of DIF analyses for the review and refinement of personnel tests.[43]

Because DIF analyses function in this way, it is possible that, even if 20% of minority group members could answer a particular item correctly while 50% of the whites could answer the item correctly (a large, 30% score gap between the two groups), the item might still escape a DIF designation. A DIF designation, however, would occur if the minority group and whites scored closely overall on the test as groups (e.g., 55% and 60% respectively), but scored this divergently on a specific test item.

Consider a fifty-item word problem test that measures basic math skills. Assume it was administered to one hundred men and one hundred women and that the men and women had similar overall scores. Forty-nine of the fifty items measure math skills using common, everyday situations encountered by men and women alike. One of the items, however, measures math skills using a football example:

> You are the quarterback on a football team. It is 4th down with 11 yards to go and you are on your own 41-yard line. You were about to throw a 30-yard pass to a receiver who would have been tackled immediately, but instead you were sacked on the 32-yard line. What is the difference between the yardage that you could have gained (had your pass been caught) versus how much you actually lost?

Does this test item measure some level of basic math? Yes, however, to arrive at the correct answer (39 yards), a test taker needs to use both math skills and football knowledge. Unless football knowledge is related to the job for which this test is being used, this item would probably show bias (via the DIF analysis) against individuals who are not familiar with football.

There are numerous methodologies available for conducting DIF analyses. These methods vary in statistical power (the test's ability to detect a DIF item if it exists), calculation complexity, and sample size requirements. Perhaps the most widely used method is known as the Mantel-Haenszel method, which is one of the more robust and classical methods for evaluating DIF (Narayanan and Swaminathan, 1995).

Because DIF analyses rely heavily on inferential statistics, they are very dependent on sample size. As such, items flagged as DIF based on large sample sizes (e.g., more than five hundred applicants) are more reliable than those based on small sample sizes (e.g., less than one hundred or so). While testing literature provides various suggestions and guidelines for sample size requirements for these types of analyses,[44] a good baseline number of test takers for conducting DIF analyses is more than two hundred applicants in the reference group (whites or men) and at least thirty in the focal group (the minority group of interest).

DIF analyses provide the most accurate results on tests that measure the same or highly-related KSAPCs, also known as having high test reliability. For example, if a fifty-item test contains twenty-five items measuring math skills and twenty-five items measuring interpersonal abilities and, because these two test areas might not be highly inter-related, the test has low reliability, DIF analyses on such a test would be unreliable and possibly inaccurate. In these circumstances, it would be best to separate the two test areas and conduct separate DIF analyses.

Most DIF analyses result in standardized statistical values that can be used to assess varying degrees of DIF (sometimes called Z values or scores). For example, a test item with a Z value of 1.5 would constitute a lesser degree of DIF than a Z value of 3.0, and so on.

There is no firm set of rules for removing items based on DIF analyses, so this practice should be approached with caution. Before removing any item from the test based on DIF analyses, the following considerations should be made:

- *The level of DIF*: The minimum level of DIF that should be considered meaningful is a Z value of 1.645 (such values are statistically significant at the .01 level). Values exceeding 2.58 (significant at the .01 level) are even more substantial. Items that have DIF levels that exceed this value should be more closely scrutinized than items with lower levels of DIF. Items that have only marginal levels of DIF should be reevaluated in subsequent test administrations.

- *The point biserial of the item*: If the item has a very high point biserial (e.g., .30 or higher), but is flagged as DIF, one should be cautious before removing the item. Items with high point biserials tend to contribute to the overall reliability of the test. If removing the item based on a DIF analysis significantly lowers the reliability of the test, the psychometric (statistics with regard to psychological traits) quality of the test will be decreased, and removing the item is not advised.

- *The item-criterion correlation (if available)*: If the test is based on a criterion-related validity study (where test scores have been statistically related to job performance), evaluate the correlation between the particular item and the measure of job performance. For example, assume that a test consisting of thirty items has an overall correlation to job performance of .30. Then consider that one of these items is flagged as DIF when administered to an applicant pool of several hundred applicants, and this specific item has a 0 (or perhaps even a negative) correlation with job performance when evaluated based on the original validation study. Such an item may be a candidate for removal (when considered along with the other guidelines herein).[45]

- *Qualitative reasons why the item could be flagged as DIF*: Sometimes items that are flagged as DIF contain certain words, phrases, or comparisons that require culturally or group-loaded content knowledge (which is unrelated to the KSAPC of interest) to provide an adequate response (such as the football-based math item example above). In this case, it can be useful to evaluate the item alternative that the DIF group selected over the majority group (e.g., if one group selected option A with high frequency, and the other selected option C).

- *The job expert validation ratings for the item*: Is the specific aspect of the KSAPC measured by the item (not just the general KSAPC to which the item is linked) necessary for the job? Did this item receive clear, positive validation ratings from the job expert panel? If the item had an unusual number of red flags when compared to the other items that were included on the test, it may be a candidate for removal.

- *The DIF values for or against other groups*: If an item shows high levels of DIF against one group, but reverse DIF for another group, caution should be used before removing the item. However, if the group showing the high levels of DIF is based on a much larger sample size than the group with reverse DIF, a greater weight should be given to the group with the larger sample size.

- *How groups scored on the subscales of the test*: DIF analyses assume that the test is measuring a single attribute or dimension (or multiple dimensions that are highly correlated). However, sometimes groups score differently on various subscales on a test, and these differences can be the reason that items are flagged for DIF (i.e., rather than the item itself being DIF against the group, it may only be flagged as DIF because it is part of a subscale on which subgroups significantly differ). For example, consider a test with the following characteristics: high overall internal consistency (reliability of .90) and two subscales: Scale A and Scale B. Assume that the average score for men is 65% on Scale A, 75% on Scale B, and 70% overall. The average score for women is 70% overall, but they have opposite scale scores compared to men (75% on Scale A and 65% on Scale B). Then assume that a DIF analysis with all items included showed that one item on Scale B was DIF against women. In this case, it would be useful to remove all items from Scale A and rerun the DIF analysis with only Scale B items included to determine if the item was still DIF against women. This process effectively controls for the advantage that women had on the overall test because of their higher score on Scale A.

For further help evaluating whether or not to remove an item due to DIF, consider the following excerpt from *Hearn v. City of Jackson* (2003) where DIF was being considered for a job-knowledge test:

> Plaintiffs suggest in their post-trial memorandum that the test is subject to challenge on the basis that [the employer] failed to perform a DIF analysis to determine whether, and if so on which items, blacks performed more poorly than whites, so that an effort could have been made to reduce adverse impact by eliminating those items on which blacks performed more poorly.... Dr. Landy testified that the consensus of professional opinion is that DIF modification of tests is not a good idea because it reduces the validity of the examination.... Dr. Landy explained: The problem with DIF is, suppose one of those items is a knowledge item and has to do with an issue like Miranda or an issue in the preservation of evidence or a hostage situation. You are going to take that item out only because whites answer it more correctly than blacks do, in spite of the fact that you would really want a sergeant to know this [issue] because the sergeant is going to supervise. A police officer is going to count on that officer to tell him or her, what to do.

So you are reducing the validity of the exam just for the sake of making sure that there are no items in which whites and blacks do differentially, or DIF, and he is assuming that the reason that 65 percent of the blacks got it right and 70 percent of the whites got it right was that it is an unfair item rather than, hey, maybe two or three whites or two or three blacks studied more or less that section of general orders.

Certainly this excerpt provides good arguments against discarding items based only on DIF analyses for job-knowledge tests. Tests measuring skills and abilities, however, may be more prone to DIF issues. These issues should be carefully considered before removing items from a test.

Test-Level Analyses

There are essentially two types of overall, test-level analyses: descriptive and psychometric. Descriptive analyses pertain to the overall statistical characteristics of the test, such as the average (mean), dispersion of scores (SD), and others. The psychometric analyses evaluate whether the test is working effectively (e.g., test reliability). The following sections discuss each of these.

Descriptive Test Analyses

The two primary descriptive types of test analyses are the mean (mathematical average) and SD (as previously mentioned, SD is the average dispersion or spread of the test scores around the mean). Only a very brief mention of these two concepts will be provided here.

The test mean shows the average score level of the applicants who took the test. Note that this does not have any bearing whatsoever on whether the applicant pool is qualified (at least the mean by itself does not). While the mean can be a useful statistic for evaluating the overall test results, it should be given less consideration when evaluating mastery-based certification, or licensing tests (because certain score levels are needed for passing the test, irrespective of the fluctuation in score averages based on various applicant groups).

As previously mentioned, the SD of the test is a statistical unit showing the average score dispersion of the overall test scores and is also useful for understanding the characteristics of the applicant pool. Typically, 68% of applicant scores will be contained within one SD above and below the test mean, 95% will be contained within two, and 99% within three. The SD can be used to evaluate whether the applicants, as a whole, are scoring too high or low on the test (hence the test is losing out on valuable information about test takers because they are magnetized to one extreme of the distribution).

The mean and SD are sometimes inappropriately used for setting cutoff scores.[46] Test developers are encouraged to use these two statistics for mostly informative, rather than instructive, purposes.

Psychometric Analyses

Like item-level analyses, numerous analyses can be done to evaluate the quality of the overall test. This discussion will be limited to the most frequently used, essential analyses for written tests, which include common forms of test reliability and the SEM. Two other advanced psychometric concepts that pertain mostly to mastery-based tests (tests used with a pass/fail cutoff based on a pre-set level of proficiency required for the job) will also be discussed at the end of this section: Decision Consistency Reliability (DCR) and Kappa Coefficients.

Test Reliability

Test reliability pertains to the consistency of applicant scores. A highly reliable test is one that measures a one-dimensional or inter-related KSAPC in a consistent way. There are several factors that can have a significant impact on the reliability of a written test; however, the most important factor is whether the items on the test hang together statistically. The items on a test need to be highly inter-correlated for a test to have high overall reliability. The Uniform Guidelines and professional standards provide no minimum thresholds for what constitutes acceptable levels of reliability. The US Department of Labor has provided the following general guidelines (2000).

Table 6-9. Guidelines for Interpreting Test Reliability

Guidelines for Interpreting Test Reliability	
Reliability Value	**Interpretation**
.90 and up	Excellent
.80–.89	Good
.70–.79	Adequate
Below .70	May have limited applicability

Perhaps the most common type of reliability analysis used for written tests is Cronbach's Alpha. This method is widely incorporated in statistical and psychometric software because it provides a highly accurate measure regarding the consistency of applicant scores. Cronbach's Alpha can be used for polytomous items, which are items that have more than one point value.

The Kuder-Richardson 20 (KR-20) formula is very similar to Cronbach's Alpha, but can only be used for dichotomously-scored items (items which have only two possible outcomes: correct or incorrect). The Kuder-Richardson 21 (KR-21) formula is another method for evaluating the overall consistency of a test. It is typically more conservative than Cronbach's Alpha and is calculated by considering only each applicant's total score (whereas the Cronbach's Alpha method takes item-level data into consideration).

Standard Error of Measurement (SEM)

To a certain extent, test reliability exists so that the SEM can be calculated. The two go hand in hand. The (traditional) SEM can be calculated easily by multiplying the SD of the test by the square root of one minus the reliability of the test. This can be calculated in Microsoft Excel as: =SD*(SQRT(1-Reliability)), where SD is the standard deviation of overall applicant test scores and Reliability is the test's level of reliability (using Cronbach's Alpha, KR-20, or the KR-21 formula, etc.).

The SEM provides a confidence interval of an applicant's true score around his or her obtained score. An applicant's true score represents his or her true, actual ability level on the overall test, whereas an applicant's obtained score represents the score that they just happened to obtain on the day the test was given. SEMs help testing professionals understand that if the applicant so much as sneezes during a hypothetical second test administration of an equally difficult test, his or her score could be lower than that obtained on the first administration. Likewise, if the applicant had a better night's sleep for the second administration, his or her score could possibly be higher than the first administration.

How this concept translates into testing is relatively straightforward. After the SEM has been calculated, it can be used to install boundaries for where each applicant's true abilities lie on the test. Assume the SEM for a written test is 3.0. This means that an applicant who scores 50 on the test most likely, with 68% confidence, has a true score ranging between 47 and 53 (one SEM, or 3.0 points, above and below his or her obtained score). Using two SEMs (or 6 points above and below his or her obtained score) provides a 95% likelihood of including a score that represents his or her true ability level. Using three SEMs provides 99% confidence.

There is one small limitation with the traditional SEM discussed above (the one calculated using the formula above). This limitation occurs because a test's reliability typically changes throughout the distribution. In other words, the reliability of the highest scorers on the test is sometimes different than the average, as well as from the lowest scorers. This is where the CSEM comes in.

Conditional Standard Error of Measurement (CSEM)

The Standards require the consideration of the CSEM when setting cutoff scores (as opposed to the traditional SEM).

The traditional SEM represents the SD of an applicant's true score (the score that represents the applicant's actual ability level) around his or her obtained (or actual) score. The traditional SEM considers the entire range of test scores when calculated. Because the traditional SEM considers the entire range of scores, its accuracy and relevance are limited when evaluating the reliability and consistency of test scores within a certain range of the score distribution.

Most test score distributions have scores bunched in the middle and spread out through the low and high range of the distribution. Those applicants who score in the lowest range of the distribution lower the overall test reliability (hence affecting the size of the SEM) by adding chance variance caused by guessing and by not possessing high enough levels of the measured KSAPC to contribute to the true score variance of the test. High scorers can also lower the overall reliability (and similarly affect the size of the SEM) because high-scoring applicants possess exceedingly high levels of the KSAPC being measured, which can also reduce the true variance included in the test score range. Figure 6-1 shows how the SEM is not constant throughout a score distribution (this chart is derived from data provided in Lord, 1984).

Figure 6-1. Standard Error of Measurement (SEM) by Score Level

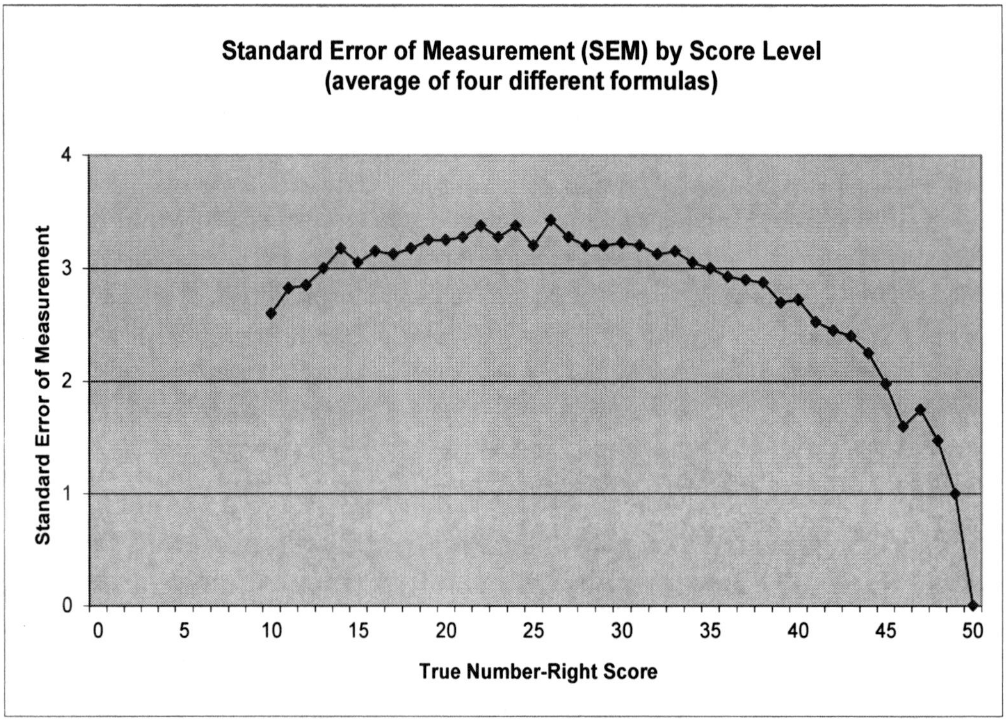

Standard Error of Measurement (SEM) by Score Level
(average of four different formulas)

Because the traditional SEM considers the average reliability of scores throughout the entire range of scores, it is less precise when considering the scores of a particular section of the score distribution. When tests are used for human resource decisions, the entire score range is almost never the central concern. Typically in human resource settings, only a certain range of scores is considered, usually those scores at or near the cutoff score, or the scores that will be included in a banding or ranking procedure.

The CSEM attempts to avoid the limitations of the SEM by considering only the score range of interest when calculating its value. By only considering the scores around the cutoff score value, the CSEM is the most accurate estimate of the reliability dynamics of the test that exist around the cutoff score.

In addition to the psychometric reasons behind the curved slope of the CSEM (as displayed by Figure 6-1), there are intuitive reasons behind the phenomena. A person who obtains a perfect or near-perfect score (95%–100%) on a multiple-choice knowledge test will almost always repeat such a score if retested. His or her high ability level will almost always be reflected on the test because his or her true score is naturally very high. Hypothetically, such a person will likely repeat his or her score if the test is administered numerous times. However, someone who scores in the middle of a distribution knows some concepts measured by the test but not others. If this person repeatedly takes the test, a greater degree of score variation will occur. This person's score will reflect some guessing on concepts he or she does not know well, certainty on those he or she does, and variance in between. The person who scores low on the test (at or slightly above the chance score of the test that could be obtained by merely guessing) would hypothetically repeat scores on the test that vary widely, with some total scores reflecting more luck than others, but with every total score being driven more by chance than true ability level.

These three hypothetical examples—the high-scoring, middle-scoring, and low-scoring test takers—reflect why the CSEM is smallest in the high score range, moderately sized in the mid-test range, and typically largest in the lowest parts of the score distribution. Several methods are available for calculating the CSEM. The TVAP system provides a similar and defensible way for calculating the CSEM.

Psychometric Analyses for Mastery-Based Tests

Tests that require predetermined levels of proficiency that are based on some job-related requirements are mastery-based tests. Mastery-based tests are used to classify applicants as masters or non-masters, or those who have enough competency or do not have enough competency, with respect to the KSAPCs being measured by the test (see Chapter 3 and Standard 14.15 of the Standards [1999]). Helpful statistics for mastery-based tests are DCR and Kappa Coefficients.

Decision Consistency Reliability (DCR)

DCR is perhaps the most important type of reliability to consider when interpreting reliability and cutoff score effectiveness for mastery-based tests. DCR attempts to answer the following question regarding a mastery-level cutoff on a test: "If the test was hypothetically administered to the same group of applicants a second time, how consistently would the applicants who passed the first time (classified as 'masters') pass the test again if they took it a second time?" Similarly, DCR attempts to answer: "How consistently would the applicants who failed the test the first time (classified as 'non-masters') fail the test if they took it a second time?" This type of reliability is different than internal consistency reliability (e.g., Cronbach's Alpha, KR-21), which considers the consistency of the test internally, without respect to the consistency with which the cutoff classifies applicants as masters and non-masters.

One very important characteristic about DCR is that it is inherently different than the other forms of reliability discussed previously. Because DCR pertains to the consistency of classification of the test, which is an action of the test (rather than an internal characteristic of the test which is what the other reliability types reveal), its value cannot be used in the classical SEM formula.

Calculating DCR is beyond the built-in commands available in most spreadsheet programs, but DCR can be calculated using the methods described in Subkoviak (1988) and Peng and Subkoviak (1980). DCR values between .75 and .84 can be considered limited; values between .85 and .90 can be considered good; and values higher than .90 can be considered excellent (Subkoviak, 1988).

Kappa Coefficients

A Kappa Coefficient explains how consistently the test classifies masters and non-masters beyond what could be expected by chance. This is essentially a measure of utility for the test. Calculating Kappa Coefficients also requires advanced statistical software or programming. For mastery-based tests, Kappa Coefficients exceeding .31 indicate adequate levels of effectiveness and levels of .42 and higher are good (Subkoviak, 1988).

Using Selection Procedures: Cutoffs, Banding, and Ranking

A perfectly valid selection procedure can be invalidated through improper use. Validation has to do with the interpretation of scores. A valid selection procedure produces scores that can be informative in both absolute and relative terms. A person who scores 90% on a written test absolutely answered about nine out of each set of ten questions correctly. Essentially, he or she answered just about every test item correctly. But what if he or she scored in the lowest 10% of all test takers (i.e., about 90% of the applicants scored higher)? This paints a completely different picture. Relative to the other applicants, he or she scored very low. Interpretation at this point can be difficult: was it the test? Was it the relative abilities of the test takers? Or are there other factors at play?

Scores on a selection procedure should be used in such a fashion that the validation evidence supports the way the selection procedure interpreted them. If classifying applicants into two groups—qualified and unqualified—is the end goal, the test should be used on a pass/fail basis. If the objective is to make relative distinctions between substantially and equally qualified applicants, then banding is the approach that should be used. Ranking should be used if the goal is to make decisions on an applicant-by-applicant basis (making sure that the requirements for ranking discussed in this chapter are addressed). If an overall picture of each applicant's combined mix of KSAPCs is desired, then a weighted and combined selection process should be used.

For each of these procedures, different types of validation evidence should be gathered to justify the corresponding manner in which the scores will be interpreted. Steps that can be taken to develop and justify each procedure are explained herein.

Developing Valid Cutoff Scores

Few things can be as frustrating as being the applicant who scored 69.9% on a test with a cutoff of 70%. Actually, there is one thing worse: finding out that the employer elected to use 70% as a cutoff on the basis that 70% seemed like a good, fair place to set the cutoff, without actually validating the cutoff score. Arbitrary cutoffs simply do not make sense, neither academically nor practically. Further, they can incense applicants who might come to realize that a meaningless standard in the selection process has been used to make very meaningful decisions about their lives and careers.

For these reasons, and because the US courts have frequently rejected arbitrary cutoffs that have adverse impact, it is essential that practitioners use best practices when developing cutoffs. When it comes to best practices for developing cutoffs, there is perhaps none better than the modified Angoff method.[47] The Angoff (1971) method makes good practical sense, job experts can readily understand it, applicants can be convinced of its validity, the courts have regularly endorsed it,[48] and it stands up to academic scrutiny.

Job experts review each item on a written test and provide their best estimate on the percentage of minimally-qualified applicants they believe would answer the item correctly (i.e., each item is assigned a percentage value). These ratings are averaged, and a valid cutoff for the test can be developed. The modified Angoff method adds a slight variation: after the test has been administered, the cutoff level set using the method above is lowered by one, two, or three CSEMs to adjust for the unreliability of the test.

The Uniform Guidelines require that pass/fail cutoffs should be "set so as to be reasonable and consistent with the normal expectations of acceptable proficiency in the workforce" (Section 5H). The modified Angoff method addresses this requirement on an item-by-item basis.

The modified Angoff method can be used for several types of selection procedures but is perhaps most widely used for written tests. The complete process for developing a cutoff using this method is described below.

Steps for Developing and Using the Modified Angoff Cutoff

The following steps are offered to develop and use a cutoff for a written test with the modified Angoff method. (It is critical that all test items have been validated before completing these steps—see Chapter 3 for the steps required for validating written test items.)

1. Select a panel of four to twelve[49] job experts who are truly experts in the content area and are diverse in terms of ethnicity, gender, geography, seniority (use a minimum of one year's experience and a maximum of five years),[50] and functional areas of the target position. Supervisors and trainers can also be included.

2. Provide a copy of the job analysis for each job expert. Be sure that the job analysis itemizes the various job duties and KSAPCs that are important or critical to the job.

3. Make a copy of the test for each job expert and stamp all tests and keys with a numbered control stamp (so that each job expert is assigned a numbered test and key). The answer key may also be provided to job experts; however, they should be urged to assess the difficulty level of the item without readily referencing the key. In some situations, masking the answer key from the job experts can help reduce the potential for upward rating bias.[51]

4. Explain the confidential nature of the workshop and the overall goals and outcomes and ask the job experts to sign confidentiality agreements. Also, explain the overall test development and validation steps, including which steps have been completed so far and which still remain to be completed.

5. Review the mechanics of a test item with the job expert panel, including the item stem (the part of the item that asks the question), alternates (all choices including the correct answer [key]), distractors (incorrect alternatives), and answer key. Also review any source linkage documentation for the items (for job-knowledge tests where the correct answers are located in a book or manual).

6. Facilitate a discussion with the job expert panel to clarify and define the concept of a minimally-qualified applicant. This is perhaps the most important part of this process because it will set the stage for the remaining steps that will

ultimately calibrate the test. The definition should be limited to an applicant who possesses the necessary, baseline levels of the KSAPC, as measured by the test item to successfully perform the first day (before training) on the job. It is sometimes useful to ask the job experts to imagine one hundred minimally-qualified applicants in the room (in the various states that an applicant can be) and ask, "How many of the one hundred applicants do you believe will answer this item correctly?"

7. Ask job experts to provide their ratings regarding the percentage of minimally-qualified applicants they believe will answer the test item correctly. Warn them against providing ratings below a chance score (50% for true/false items; 25% for multiple choice items with four alternatives; 20% for items with five). In addition, job experts should not assign ratings of 100% because this rating allows no room for error.

8. Allow the job experts to continue rating the first five test items and then stop. Select one of the first five test items as a group discussion item. Ask each of the job experts to share his or her percentage ratings for the item. Allow the job experts to debate their ratings. This will help centralize the panel and minimize any extreme outliers before they rate the remaining items. It is acceptable to stimulate the job experts by discussing and contrasting their ratings, though the facilitator should neither require nor coerce any job expert to make any changes. The facilitator and the job experts can argue, discuss, and challenge any individual job expert rating during group discussion; however, in the end, each job expert should cast his or her own vote.

9. Collect all rating surveys and remind job experts of the confidential nature of their workshop participation.

10. Input and double-check all job expert ratings.

11. Detect and remove outlier job experts from the data set. Experience shows that one or more outliers exist in almost every job expert panel. Outliers are raters who purposefully rate items too low (in interest of lowering the standard), too high (to raise the standard), or just plain randomly. Statistical control processes should be used to detect each of these potential rating biases, and the identified job expert's data set should be removed before the final cutoff level is set. While a variety of techniques is available to accomplish this goal, here are two that can be readily computed using spreadsheet programs as described below:

   a. To check for a job expert whose ratings are systematically too low or too high compared to the rest of the panel, calculate the average and SD of the job expert averages for all items on the test (an average of their averages). Then remove any job expert whose average ratings are 1.645[52] SDs above or below the average of all job experts.

b. To detect job experts who provided random responses, or responses that were not congruent (to an extent) with the ratings of the other job experts, create an inter-correlation matrix (using the =PEARSON command in Excel) for all job experts on the panel. Look for job experts who were (a) not correlated with their peers (or less correlated than most other raters), and/or (b) not correlated with the average rating of all raters (by averaging the ratings for each item across all raters), and remove them from the data set (judgment will need to be used at this step to make considerations for the number of job experts, number of items rated, statistical power, etc.).

Because removing job experts using step a or b above will change the data set (possibly creating new problems with the remaining data), it is recommended to only complete this iteration once, and to be sure to complete the steps in order (a first, then b).

12. Calculate a pre-administration cutoff percentage (also called an "unmodified Angoff score" because it has not yet been reduced using the CSEM) with the remaining data. The pre-administration cutoff percentage score is the average of the job expert panel's average ratings for each item on the final test. Each item's average percentage rating receives equal weight in the calculation of this score—if only two job experts rated an item, the item's average is only based on two values but the item is given equal weight to the item rated by the entire panel.

13. Administer the test and remove any items (if necessary) based on item- or test-level analyses. If an item is removed from the test, also remove that item's average percentage rating from the calculation of the pre-administration cutoff percentage.

14. Calculate the three post-administration cutoff raw score options by (1) multiplying the pre-administration cutoff percentage by the number of items in the test (e.g., 76.7% * 90 items = 69.03 of the 90 items answered correctly); (2) identifying the Estimated True Score (ETS) associated with this raw score, using the formula: $ETS = ((X-M) * r_{xx} + M)$ where X is the score, M is the average test score of all examinees, and r_{xx} is the reliability of the test; (3) "flooring" this score to the lowest value (because test takers cannot achieve fraction scores on written tests); and finally (4) reducing this value by one, two, or three CSEMs. For example, using the example above and a test with a mean of 60 and reliability of .90, the ETS would be 68.127, which is floored to a score of 68. If the CSEM at the score of 68 was 3.5, the three cutoff score options (A, B, C) would be option A: 64 (68 - 3.5 = 64.5, which floors to 64); option B: 61 (68 - (3.5 * 2 = 7); and option C: 57 (68 - (3.5 * 3 = 10.5) = 57.5, which floors to 57.

This process provides three viable cutoff score options for the test. In the US Supreme Court decision made in *United States v. South Carolina* (1978), five statistical and human factors were considered when deciding whether to use one, two, or three SEMs when setting the final cutoff score:

- Size of the SEM. Using the CSEM is recommended over the traditional SEM because the CSEM considers the error variance (unreliability) only for test takers around the cutoff score, which is the area of decision-making interest. Large SEMs indicate low test reliability and/or high levels of variance in the applicant pool.

- Possibility of sampling error in the study (this relates to the number of job experts who served on the cutoff development panel). Panels with only a few job experts raise concern based on this factor.

- Consistency of the results (internal comparisons of the panel results). Panels that included biased job experts raise concern here (only if they were not removed using the proposed steps above).

- Supply and demand for teachers in each specialty field (this pertains to the demand for workers needed in the work force).

- Racial composition of the teacher force (the levels of adverse impact on each of the three cutoff options should be considered).

While these factors were based upon the specific needs and circumstances in *United States v. South Carolina*, they provide some useful considerations for employers when setting cutoff scores.

An additional (optional) step can be taken to further evaluate and possibly refine the final cutoff score. This step has to do with an evaluation of the possible upward rating bias that sometimes occurs with job expert rating panels. This step is useful because, in some situations, job expert panels set the bar too high. This upward bias tendency that is sometimes observed does not rule out the opposite, where a rater panel underestimates the ideal minimum competency level. However, it has been our experience that rating biases of the overestimation type are more common than those of the underestimation nature.

While there are several viable theories that may explain why this phenomenon can occur with rating panels, one particular theory seems to provide a practical explanation—the Conscious Competence Theory (sometimes also called the Four Stages of Learning theory). This theory, which has been attributed to psychologist Abraham Maslow, explains how people learn in four progressive stages:

1. Unconscious Incompetence (you do not know that you do not know something); to,

2. Conscious Incompetence (you are now aware that you are incompetent at something); to,

3. Conscious Competence (you develop a skill in that area but have to think about it); to,

4. Unconscious Competence (you are good at it and it now comes naturally).

These four learning stages have been widely adopted in both theory and practice in the educational, psychological, and organizational behavior fields since their inception. It is the fourth stage (Unconscious Competence) that may cause some of the upward bias sometimes observed in rating panels. This is because individuals who have had so much practice with a particular skill—to the point where it becomes second nature and can be performed easily without intense concentration—can sometimes underestimate how long it took them to master the skill when they first started in the position. This may cause them to overestimate the percentage of qualified applicants who may be able to answer the test question on the first day of the job.

Common examples of skills that can be attained at this fourth level include driving, sports activities, typing, manual dexterity tasks, listening, and communicating. For example, performing a U-turn is second nature to most people who have been driving for several years. In fact, many experienced drivers may not even recall ever having to acquire this skill, but in actuality many experienced drivers initially had to work hard at this skill until it was mastered.

This issue can create an upward bias when applying minimum passing score recommendations. Some raters might now be able to teach others the target skill, although after some time of being unconsciously competent, the person might actually have difficulty explaining exactly how they perform a particular skill because the skill has become largely instinctual. This arguably gives rise to the need for long-standing unconscious competence to be checked periodically against new standards.

Fortunately, the extent to which this possible bias may exist can be evaluated statistically. This can be completed by statistically comparing how the rating panels' recommended cutoff score related to the scores of the test takers who scored in the region of the recommended cutoff score.[53] Specifically, an item-by-item comparison can be made between each item's difficulty level (the percentage of test takers who obtained scores in the passing range who answered the item correctly) and the item's average Angoff rating. For example, if the item difficulty (based on applicants in the passing score zone) of a particular item is 55%, but the average Angoff rating from the job expert panel is 80%, a 25% potential overestimate gap exists. The opposite would, of course, suggest a potential underestimate made by the job expert panel. And, if this trend ensues throughout the majority of items, an overall upward rating bias may exist.

One way to investigate whether there is a trend of overestimates is to evaluate the distribution skew of the gaps between item difficulties and Angoff ratings. Skew is a statistical indicator that reflects whether the distribution of the data is symmetrical (uniformly distributed with an equal number of values above and below the average of the distribution). The skew statistic can be computed in Excel by applying the =SKEW formula to the column containing the difference values between the Angoff ratings and item difficulties. If the skewness statistic is zero (0), the data are perfectly symmetrical. As a general guideline, if the skewness statistic is less than -1 or greater than +1, the distribution is highly skewed. If skewness is between -1 and -½ or between +½ and +1, the distribution is moderately skewed. If skewness is between -½ and +½, the distribution is approximately symmetric. This skewness statistic can be applied to the difference values computed by obtaining the difference between Angoff ratings and the item difficulties. If the Angoff rating is subtracted from the item difficulties, positive skew values would reveal that there is a disproportionately high number of test items with positive values indicating that items were potentially over-rated by the raters. Negative skew values indicate the opposite.

The standard error of the skew can then be computed in Excel (using the formula: =SQRT(6/N), where N is the number of difference values). Then multiply this value by 2. If the resulting value exceeds 2.0, the skewness is significant and an adjustment to the cutoff score should be made (Tabachnick and Fidell, 1996).

There are two types of possible adjustments that can be made to the cutoff score if the skewness test is significant. The first adjustment can be made by reducing each over-rated item's Angoff rating to the lower confidence boundary of the item's Angoff rating by multiplying the SE Mean Angoff rating[54] by 1.96 for each over-rated item. For example, if the average Angoff rating for an item is 85% and the SE Mean is 3%, multiply 3% by 1.96 (5.88%) and subtract this value from 85% to arrive at the new Angoff rating for that item (79.12%).

If the skewness test results exceed 3.0, consider using a more robust adjustment that can be computed by reducing the cutoff score to the lower confidence boundary of the raters' overall cutoff score. This can be accomplished by multiplying the SED of the rater panel[55] by 1.96, and then subtracting this value from the cutoff score.

Setting Cutoffs That Are Higher Than the Minimum Level Established by the Modified Angoff Method

What should be done if the employer cannot feasibly hire all applicants who pass the validated cutoff score? Theoretically speaking, all applicants who pass the modified Angoff cutoff are qualified; however, if the employer simply cannot hire the number of applicants who pass the given cutoff, two options are available.

The first option is to use a cutoff that is higher than the three cutoff options calculated above. If this option is used, the Uniform Guidelines are clear that the degree of adverse impact should be considered (see Sections 3B and 5H). One method for setting a higher cutoff is to subtract one SED from the highest score in the distribution, and pass all applicants in this score band. Using the SED in this process helps ensure that all applicants within the band are substantially equally qualified. Additional bands can be created by subtracting one SED from the score immediately below the band for the next group and repeating this process until the first cutoff score option is reached (one CSEM below the cutoff score). This represents the distinguishing line between the qualified and unqualified applicants.

While this option may be useful for obtaining a smaller group of applicants who pass the cutoff score and are substantially equally qualified, a second option is strict rank ordering. However, strict rank ordering is not typically advised on written tests because of the high levels of adverse impact that are likely to result. To hire or promote applicants in strict rank order on a score list, the employer should be careful to ensure that the criteria discussed in the ranking section are sufficiently addressed.

Banding

In some circumstances, applicants are rank-ordered on a selection procedure, and hiring decisions between applicants are based upon score differences at the one-hundredth or one-thousandth decimal place (e.g., applicant A who scored 89.189 is hired before applicant B who scored 89.188, etc.). The troubling issue with this practice is that if the selection procedure were administered a second time, it is just as possible that applicants A and B could very likely change places. In fact, if the reliability of the selection procedure was low and the SD was large, these two applicants could, in fact, be separated by several whole points rather than mere fractions.

Banding addresses this issue by using the SED to group applicants into substantially equally qualified score bands. The SED is a tool that can be used by practitioners for setting a confidence interval around scores that are substantially equal. Viewed another way, it can be used for determining scores in a distribution that represent meaningfully different levels of the KSAPCs measured by the selection procedure.

For example, assume a selection procedure with a possible score range of 0 to 100 and a SED of four. If the highest scoring applicant obtained a score of 99, subtracting one SED from this score (99 - 4) arrives at a score of 95, which can be considered the first meaningful stopping place in the distribution of scores. That is, the applicant who scored 99 and the applicant who scored 94 have different ability levels, but the applicant who scored 99 and the applicant who scored 95 do not. Different band widths can be applied (by using one, two, or three SEDs) that provide different confidence levels surrounding the meaningful differences between scores. Note, however, that some banding techniques require a bidirectional consideration (higher and lower scorers) of the confidence intervals surrounding scores.

Banding has been a hotly debated issue in the personnel field.[56] Proponents of strict rank ordering argue that making hiring decisions in rank-order preserves meritocracy and ultimately ensures a more qualified workforce. Supporters of banding argue that, because tests cannot adequately distinguish between small score differences, practitioners should remain blind to miniscule score differences between applicants who are within the same band. They also argue that the practice of banding will almost always produce less adverse impact than strict rank ordering.[57] While these two perspectives may differ, various types of score banding procedures have been successfully litigated and supported in court (such as *Officers for Justice v. Civil Service Commission*, 1996) with one exception being the decision to band after a test has been administered, when the only reason for banding was to reduce adverse impact (*Ricci v. DeStefano*, 2009). Otherwise, banding remains an effective tool that can be used in most personnel situations.

Ranking

The idea of hiring applicants in strict order from the top of the list to the last applicant above the cutoff score is a practice that has roots back to the origins of the merit-based civil service system. The limitation with ranking, as discussed above, is that the practice can treat applicants whose scores are actually close to identical as if they were meaningfully different. The SEM shows the degree to which scores would likely shuffle if the selection procedure was hypothetically administered a second time.

Because of these limitations, the Uniform Guidelines and the courts have presented rather stringent requirements surrounding the practice of strict rank ordering. These requirements are provided below, along with some specific recommendations on the criteria to consider before using a selection procedure to rank order applicants.

Section 14C9 of the Uniform Guidelines states:

> If a user can show, by a job analysis or otherwise, that a higher score on a content valid selection procedure is likely to result in better job performance, the results may be used to rank persons who score above minimum levels. Where a selection procedure supported solely or primarily by content validity is used to rank job candidates, the selection procedure should measure those aspects of performance which differentiate among levels of job performance.

Performance-differentiating KSAPCs distinguish between acceptable and above-acceptable on-the-job performance. Differentiating KSAPCs can be identified either absolutely or relatively using the Best-Worker rating discussed in Chapter 3. A strict rank ordering process should not be used on a selection procedure that measures KSAPCs that are only needed at minimum levels on the job and do not distinguish between acceptable and above-acceptable job performance (see Uniform Guidelines Questions and Answers, Supplement number 62).

Content validity evidence to support ranking can be established by linking the parts of a selection procedure to job duties and/or KSAPCs that are performance differentiating.[58] So, if a selection procedure is linked to a job duty and/or KSAPC that is either absolutely or relatively "performance differentiating" (with an average job expert Best-Worker rating that is one SD above the average Best-Worker rating or higher when compared to all other duties and/or KSAPCs), some support is provided for using the selection procedure as a ranking device.

While the Best-Worker rating provides some support for using a selection procedure as a ranking device, some additional factors should be considered before making a decision to use a selection procedure in a strict rank-ordered fashion:

1. Is there score dispersion in the distribution (or a wide variance of scores)? Rank ordering is usually not preferred if the applicant scores are tightly bunched together[59] because such scores are tied to an even greater extent than if they were more evenly distributed. One way to evaluate the dispersion of scores is to use the CSEM. Using the CSEM, the employer can evaluate if the score dispersion is adequately spread out within the relevant range of scores when compared to other parts of the score distribution. For example, if the CSEM is very small (e.g., two) in the range of scores where the strict rank ordering will occur (e.g., 95–100), but is very broad throughout the other parts of the score distribution (e.g., double or triple the size), the score dispersion in the relevant range of interest (e.g., 95–100) may not be sufficiently high to justify this criteria.

2. Does the selection procedure have high reliability? Typically, reliability coefficients should be .85 to .90 or higher for using the results in strict rank order.[60] If a selection procedure is not reliable (or consistent) enough to separate candidates based upon very small score differences, it should not be used in such a way that small differences between candidates are considered meaningful.

While the guidelines above should be considered when choosing a rank ordering or pass/fail strategy for a selection procedure, the extent to which the test measures KSAPCs and/or job duties[61] that are performance differentiating should be the primary consideration.

Employers using a selection procedure that is based on criterion-related validity evidence have more flexibility to use ranking than with selection procedures based on content validity. This is because criterion-related validity demonstrates scientifically what content validity can only speculate is occurring between the selection procedure and job performance. Criterion-related validity (see Chapter 2 for a more detailed discussion) provides a correlation coefficient that represents the strength or degree of correlation relationship between some aspects of job performance and the selection procedure.

While the courts have regularly endorsed criterion-related validity studies, they have placed some minimum thresholds for the correlation value necessary (about .30 or higher) for strict rank ordering on a selection procedure based on criterion-related validity:

- *Brunet v. City of Columbus* (1993). This case involved an entry-level firefighter Physical Capacities Test (PCT) that had adverse impact against women. The court stated, "The correlation coefficient for the overall PCT is .29. Other courts have found such correlation coefficients to be predictive of job performance, thus indicating the appropriateness of ranking where the correlation coefficient value is .30 or better."

- *Boston Chapter, NAACP Inc. v. Beecher* (1974). This case involved an entry-level firefighter written test. Regarding the correlation values, the court stated, "The objective portion of the study produced several correlations that were statistically significant (likely to occur by chance in fewer than five of one hundred similar cases) and practically significant (correlation of +.3 or higher, thus explaining more than 9% or more of the observed variation)."

- *Clady v. County of Los Angeles* (1985). This case involved an entry-level firefighter written test. The court stated, "In conclusion, the County's validation studies demonstrate legally sufficient correlation to success at the Academy and on-the-job performance. Courts generally accept correlation coefficients above +.30 as reliable.... As a general principle, the greater the test's adverse impact, the higher the correlation which will be required."

- *Zamlen v. City of Cleveland* (1988). This case involved several different entry-level firefighter PATs that had various correlation coefficients with job performance. The judge noted that, "Correlation coefficients of .30 or greater are considered high by industrial psychologists" and set a criteria of .30 to endorse the City's option of using the PAT as a ranking device.

Weighting Selection Procedures into Combined Scores

Selection procedures can be weighted and combined into a composite score for each applicant. Typically, each selection procedure that is used to make the combined score is also used as a screening device (i.e., with a pass/fail cutoff) before including scores from applicants into the composite score. Before using a selection procedure as a pass/fail device and as part of a weighted composite, the developer should evaluate whether the KSAPCs measured by the selection procedures are performance differentiating—especially if the weighted composite will be used for ranking applicants.

There are two critical factors to consider when weighting selection procedures into composite scores: determining the weights and standardizing the scores. Developing a reliability coefficient for the final list of composite scores[62] is also a critical final step if the final scores will be banded into groups of substantially equally qualified applicants. These steps are discussed below.

Determining a set of job-related weights to use when combining selection procedures can be a sophisticated and socially sensitive issue. Not only are the statistical mechanics often complicated, but choosing one set of weights versus another can sometimes have a very significant impact on the gender and ethnic composition of those who are hired from the final applicant list. For these reasons, this topic should be approached with caution and developers should make decisions using informed judgment.

Generally speaking, weighting the selection procedures that will be combined into composite scores for each applicant can be accomplished using one of three methods: unit weighting, weighting based on criterion-related validity studies, and content-validity weighting methods.

Unit weighting is accomplished by simply allowing each selection procedure to share an equal weight in the combined score list. Surprisingly, sometimes unit weighting produces highly effective and valid results (SIOP, 2003). This is probably because each selection procedure is allowed to contribute equally to making the composite score, and no selection procedure is hampered by only contributing a small part to the final score. Using unit weighting, if there are two selection procedures, they are each weighted 50%. If there are five, each is allowed 20% weight.

If the employer is using selection procedures that are based on one or more criterion-related validity studies, the data from these studies can be used to calculate the weights for each. The steps for this method are outside the scope of this text and will not be discussed here.[63]

Using content validity methods to weight selection procedures is probably the most common practice. Sometimes practitioners get caught up in developing complicated and computationally-intensive methods for weighting selection procedures using job analysis data. Sometimes these procedures involve using complicated formulas that consider frequency and importance ratings for job duties and/or KSAPCs, and job duty/KSAPC linkages.

While this helps some practitioners feel at ease, these methods can produce misleading results. Not only that, there are easier methods available. For example, consider two KSAPCs that are equally important to the job. Now assume that one is more complex than the other, so it is divided into two KSAPCs on the job analysis, while the other (equally important) KSAPC remains in a single slot on the job analysis. When it comes time to use multiplication formulas to determine weights for the selection procedures that are linked to these KSAPCs, one is likely to receive more weight simply because it was written twice on the job analysis. The same problem exists if selection procedures are mechanically linked using job duties that have this issue.

What about just providing the list of KSAPCs to a panel of job experts and having them distribute one hundred points to indicate the relative importance of each? This method is fine, but can also present some limitations. Assume there are twenty KSAPCs and job experts assign importance points to each. Now assume that only twelve of these KSAPCs are actually tested by the set of selection procedures chosen for the weighted composite. Would the weight values turn out differently if the job experts were allowed to review the twelve remaining KSAPCs and were asked to reassign their weighting values? Most likely, yes, as illustrated in the example below:

> Ask a friend to list his or her top ten favorite ice cream flavors in no particular order. Then ask him or her to distribute one hundred points among the ten flavors, indicating the relative importance of each. Remove five ice cream flavors and have your friend distribute one hundred points to the remaining five (not considering their original weighting). The weights they assign the second time to the five remaining ice cream flavors will likely be different than the weights that would be calculated by taking their original list of ten (along with the corresponding weights of each), removing the same five ice cream flavors, then recalculating the weights by dividing the original weight of each by the new total based on only the remaining five.

Another limitation with weighting selection procedures by evaluating their relative weight from job analysis data is that different selection procedures are sometimes linked to the same KSAPC (which can make the weights no longer unique for each selection procedure and leave them convoluted with other selection procedures).

One final limitation is that selection procedures are sometimes linked to a KSAPC for collecting the weight determination but prove to be weak measures of the KSAPC (while others are strong, relevant linkages). For these reasons, there is a better way, as described below.

The following steps can be taken to develop content valid weights for selection procedures that are combined into single composite scores for each applicant:

1. Select a panel of four to twelve job experts who are truly experts in the content area and are diverse in terms of ethnicity, gender, geography, seniority (use a minimum of one year experience), and functional areas of the target position. Supervisors and trainers can also be included.

2. Provide a copy of the job analysis for each job expert. Be sure that the job analysis itemizes the various job duties and KSAPCs that are important or critical to the job.

3. Provide each job expert with a copy of each selection procedure (or a highly detailed description of the content of the selection procedure if confidentiality issues prohibit job experts from viewing actual copies). Make a copy of the selection procedure and key for each job expert and stamp with a numbered control stamp (so that each job expert is assigned a numbered set).

4. Explain the confidential nature of the workshop, the overall goals and outcomes, and ask the job experts to sign confidentiality agreements.

5. Discuss and review the content of each selection procedure and the KSAPCs measured by each with the job experts. A selection plan is helpful for this step (see Chapter 3). Also discuss the extent to which certain selection procedures may be better measures of certain KSAPCs than others. Factors such as the vulnerability of certain selection procedures to fraud, reliability issues, and others should be discussed.

6. Provide a survey to job experts that asks them to distribute one hundred points among the selection procedures that will be combined. Be sure that they consider the importance levels of the KSAPCs measured by the selection procedures and the job duties to which they are linked when completing this step.

7. Detect and remove outlier job experts from the data set (raters can be removed if their average weight rating is 1.645 SDs above or below the collective average).

8. Calculate the average weight for each selection procedure. These averages are the weights to use when combining the selection procedure into a composite score.

Standardizing Scores

Before individual selection procedures can be weighted and combined, it is absolutely crucial that they be standard scored. Standard scoring is a statistical process of normalizing scores and is a necessary step to place different selection procedures on a level playing field.

Assume a developer has two selection procedures: one with a score range of 0 to 10 and the other with a range of 0 to 50. What happens when these two selection procedures are combined? The one with a high score range will greatly overshadow the one with the smaller range. Even if two selection procedures have the same score range, they should still be standard scored. This is because if the selection procedures have different means and SDs they will produce inaccurate results when combined unless they are first standard scored.

Standardizing scores is a relatively simple practice. Converting raw scores into Z scores (a widely used form of standard scoring) can be done by simply subtracting each applicant's score from the average score of all applicants and dividing this value by the SD of all applicant total scores. After the scores for each selection procedure are standard scored, they can be multiplied by their respective weights and a final score for each applicant calculated. After this final score list has been compiled, the reliability of the new combined list can be calculated (Feldt and Brennan, 1989).

Chapter 7—Would Your Agency Survive a Legal Challenge?

A content validation model supports most tests in the public safety industry, but criterion-related validity supports some tests, such as personality tests and some types of cognitive ability tests. Tables 7-1 through 7-5 outline how the Uniform Guidelines are addressed when a department claims either type of validity in an enforcement/litigation setting.

Content Validation Checklist for Written Tests

Table 7-1. Content Validation Checklist for Written Tests

Req. #	Uniform Guidelines Requirements	Uniform Guidelines Reference
1	Does the test have sufficiently high reliability? (Generally, written tests should have reliability values that exceed .70[1] *for each section of the test that applicants are required to pass.*)	14C(5)
2	Does the test measure KSAPCs that have been rated as critical (necessary prerequisites for performance of the job) for each job that used the test? (Or, does the test measure KSAPCs that are important which are also clearly linked to critical [necessary for performance of the job] job duties, or job duties that constitute *most of the job*?)	14C(1,4,8)
3	If the test is used for testing the KSAPCs of higher-level positions, are job progression structures so established that employees will probably, within a reasonable period of time and in a majority of cases, progress to those higher level jobs?	5I
4	Does the test measure KSAPCs that are necessary on the first day of the job? (Check No if the KSAPCs measured by the test will be trained on the job or can be "learned in a brief orientation.")	14C(1), 5F, 5I(3)
5	Does the test measure KSAPCs that are *concrete and not theoretical*? (Under content validity, tests cannot measure abstract traits such as intelligence, aptitude, personality, common sense, judgment, leadership, or spatial ability, if they are not defined in concrete, observable ways.)	14C(1,4)
6	Is sufficient time allowed for nearly all applicants to complete the test?[2] (Unless the test was specifically validated with a time limit, sufficient time should be allowed for nearly all applicants to finish.)	15C(5)
7	*For tests measuring job knowledge only*: Does the test measure job-knowledge areas that need to be committed to memory? (Check No if the job-knowledge areas can be easily looked up without hindering job performance.)	15C(3), Q&A 79
8	Were alternative procedures that are "substantially equally valid," but have less adverse impact, investigated?	3B, 15B(9)

[1]US Department of Labor (2000).

[2] Crocker and Algina (1986).

Criterion-Related Validation Checklist for Written Tests

Table 7-2. Criterion-Related Validation Checklist for Written Tests

Req. #	Uniform Guidelines Requirements	Uniform Guidelines Reference
1	Is there a description of the test? Look for title, description, purpose, target population, administration, scoring, and interpretation of scores.	15B(4)
2	If the test is a combination of other tests or if the final score is derived by weighting different parts of the test or different tests, is there a description of the rationale and justification for such combination or weighting?	15B(10)
3	Does the test have sufficiently high reliability (e.g., .70[1] is desirable)?	15C(7)
4	Is there a description of the criterion measure, including the basis for its selection or development and method of collection? For ratings, look for information related to the rating form and instructions to raters.	15B(5)
5	Does the criterion (e.g., performance) measure reflect either: (a) important or critical work behaviors or outcomes as identified through a job analysis or review, or (b) an important business need, such as absenteeism, productivity, tardiness, or other?	14B(2)(3), 15B(3)
6	Is the sample size adequate for each position for which validity is being claimed? Look for evidence that the correlations between the predictor and criterion measures are sufficient for each position included in the study.	14B(1)
7	Is the study sample representative of all possible test takers? Look for evidence that the sample was chosen to include individuals of different races and gender. For concurrent validity studies, look for evidence that the sample included individuals with different amounts of experience. Where a number of jobs are studied together (e.g., a job group), look for evidence that the sample included individuals from all jobs included in the study.	14B(4)
8	Are the methods of analysis and results described? Look for a description of the method of analysis, measures of central tendency such as average scores, measures of the relationship between the predictor and criterion measures, and race/gender differences.	15B(8)
9	Is the correlation between scores on the test and the criterion statistically significant *before* applying any statistical corrections?	14B(5)
10	Is the test being used for the same jobs for which it was validated? For the same type of test takers?	14B(6), 15B(10)
11	Have steps been taken to correct for overstatement and understatement of validity findings, such as corrections for range restriction, use of large sample sizes, or cross-validation? If corrections are made, are the raw and corrected values reported?	14B(7)
12	Has the fairness of the test been examined or, if not feasible, is there a plan to conduct such a study?	14B(8)
13	Has a validation study been conducted in the last five years or, if not, is there evidence that the job has not changed since the last validity study?	5K
14	Were alternative procedures that are "substantially equally valid," but have less adverse impact, investigated?	3B, 15B(9)
15	If criterion-related validity for the test is being transported from another employer/position, were the following requirements addressed: (a) did the original validation study address Section 14B of the Guidelines; (b) are the jobs substantially the same major work behaviors (as shown by job analyses in both locations); and (c) was a fairness study conducted (if technically feasible)?	7B, 14B

[1] US Department of Labor (2000).

Validation Checklist for Structured Interviews

Table 7-3. Content Validation Checklist for Structured Interviews

Req. #	Uniform Guidelines Requirements	Uniform Guidelines Reference
1	*If multiple raters are involved in the interview administration/scoring,*[1] does the interview have sufficiently high inter-rater reliability? (Generally, interviews should have reliability values that exceed .60[2] *for each section of the interview that applicants are required to pass.*)	14C(5)
2	Does the interview measure KSAPCs that have been rated as critical (necessary prerequisites for performance of the job) for each job that used the test? (Or, does the test measure KSAPCs that are important which are also clearly linked to critical [necessary for performance of the job] job duties, or job duties that constitute *most of the job.*)	14C(1,4,8)
3	If the interview is used for testing the KSAPCs of higher-level positions, are job progression structures so established that employees will probably, within a reasonable period of time and in a majority of cases, progress to those higher level jobs?	5I
4	Does the interview measure KSAPCs that are necessary on the first day of the job? (Check No if the KSAPCs measured by the interview will be trained on the job or can be "learned in a brief orientation.")	14C(1), 5F, 5I(3)
5	Does the interview measure KSAPCs that are *concrete and not theoretical*?	14C(1,4)
6	*For interviews measuring job knowledge only*: Does the interview measure job-knowledge areas that need to be committed to memory? (Check No if the job-knowledge areas can be easily looked up without hindering job performance.)	15C(3), Q&A 79
7	Were alternative procedures that are "substantially equally valid," but have less adverse impact, investigated?	3B, 15B(9)

[1] "Internal-consistency" reliability for interviews with one or multiple raters is also important; however, inter-rater reliability sets the upper limit on reliability when multiple-rater panels are used.

[2] Most resources recommend using reliability levels of at least .70 as a baseline (e.g., US Department of Labor, 2000); however, interviews typically have lower reliability levels than written tests.

Validation Checklist for Work-Sample Tests or PATs

Table 7-4. Content Validation Checklist for Work-Sample (WS) Tests or PATs

Req. #	Uniform Guidelines Requirements	Uniform Guidelines Reference
1	Does the WS/PAT have sufficiently high reliability? (Typically, WS/PATs need to be supported using test-retest reliability, unless they have a sufficient number of scored components to be evaluated using internal consistency. Generally, WS/PATs should have reliability values that exceed .70[1] for each section of the test that applicants are required to pass.)	14C(5)
2	Does the WS/PAT measure KSAPCs that have been rated as "critical" (necessary prerequisites for performance of the job) for each job that used the test? (Or, does the test measure KSAPCs that are important, which are also clearly linked to critical [necessary for performance of the job] job duties, or job duties that constitute *most of the job*?)	14C(1,4,8)
3	If the WS/PAT is used for testing the KSAPCs of higher-level positions, are job progression structures established so that employees will probably, within a reasonable period of time and in a majority of cases, progress to those higher level jobs?	5I
4	Does the WS/PAT measure KSAPCs that are necessary on the first day of the job? (Check No if the KSAPCs measured by the WS/PAT will be trained on the job or can be "learned in a brief orientation.")	14C(1), 5F, 5I(3)
5	Does the WS/PAT measure KSAPCs that are concrete and not theoretical? Measuring general strength, fitness, or stamina cannot be supported under content validity unless they are operationally defined in terms of observable aspects of work behavior (job duties).	14C(1,4), 15C(5)
6	If the WS/PAT is designed to replicate/simulate actual work behaviors, is the manner, setting, and level of complexity highly similar to the job?	14C(4)
7	If the WS/PAT has multiple events and is scored using a time limit (e.g., all events must be completed in five minutes or faster), are the events in the WS/PAT typically performed on the job with other physically-demanding duties performed immediately prior to and after each event?	15C(5)
8	If the WS/PAT has multiple events and is scored using a time limit (e.g., all events must be completed in five minutes or faster), is speed typically important when these duties are performed on the job?	15C(5)
9	If the WS/PAT includes weight handling requirements (e.g., lifting, carrying certain objects or equipment), do they represent the weights, distances, and duration that objects/equipment are typically carried by a single person on the job?	15C(5)
10	If there are any special techniques that are learned on the job that allow current job incumbents to perform the events in the test better than an applicant could, are they demonstrated to the applicants before the test?	14C(1), 5F, 5I(3)
11	Does the WS/PAT require the same or less exertion of the applicant than is required on the job?	5H, 15C(5)
12	Were alternative procedures that are "substantially equally valid," but have less adverse impact, investigated?	3B, 15B(9)

[1] US Department of Labor (2000).

Validation Checklist for Using Test Results

Table 7-5. Validation Checklist for Using Test Results

Req. #	Uniform Guidelines Requirements	Uniform Guidelines Reference
1	If a pass/fail cutoff is used, is the cutoff "set so as to be reasonable and consistent with normal expectations of acceptable proficiency within the work force?"	5G, 5H, 15C(7)
2	If the test is ranked or banded above a minimum cutoff level and is *based on content validity*, can it be shown that either (a) applicants scoring below a certain level have little or no chance of being selected for employment, or (b) the test measures KSAPCs / job duties that are "performance differentiating?"[1]	3B, 5G, 5H, 14C(9)
3	If the test is ranked or banded above a minimum cutoff level and is based on criterion-related validity, can it be shown that either (a) applicants scoring below a certain level have little or no chance of being selected for employment, or (b) the degree of statistical correlation and the importance and number of aspects of job performance covered by the criteria clearly justify ranking rather than using the test in a way that would lower adverse impact (e.g., banding or using a cutoff)? (Tests that have adverse impact and are used to rank and that are only related to one of many job duties or aspects of job performance should be subjected to close review.)	3B, 5G, 5H, 14B(6)
4	Is the test used[2] in a way that minimizes adverse impact? (Options include different cutoff points, banding, or weighting the results in ways that are still "substantially equally valid" but reduce or eliminate adverse impact.)	3B, 5G

[1] "Performance Differentiating" KSAPCs are those that differentiate between "adequate" and "superior" job performance (see UGESP, Section 14C[9]).

[2] "Alternate uses" of a practice, procedure, or test can include different cutoff points, banding, or weighting the results in ways that are still "substantially equally valid."

Chapter 8—Lessons from the *Ricci* Case

The Ricci *Case: An Overview*

On June 29, 2009, the US Supreme Court handed down the first Title VII ruling that answers the difficult question: "Under what circumstances can an employer subject to Title VII implement otherwise prohibited disparate-treatment discrimination to avoid disparate impact liability?" When answering this question in the *Ricci* ruling, the US Supreme Court adopted a "strong-basis-in-evidence standard" as a matter of statutory construction for courts to use as a means of resolving conflicts between Title VII's disparate-treatment and disparate-impact provisions—"allowing violations of one in the name of compliance with the other only in certain, narrow circumstances" (2009).[64]

Twenty years prior to the *Ricci* case, the US Supreme Court codified the strong-basis-in-evidence standard in *Richmond v. Croson* (1989)—a concept that first originated three years earlier in *Wygant v. Jackson Board of Education* (1986) by Justice Powell. Both of these cases laid down legal concepts that were relevant to the *Ricci* context in ways that will be fully explored in this Chapter—defining how the strong-basis-in-evidence standard applies to various personnel actions and diversity initiatives.

The context of the *Ricci v. DeStefano* (2009) case involved the City of New Haven's (Connecticut) firefighter promotional practices. The foundation for the City's selection procedure is an agreement with its firefighters' union that only a written test and an oral interview will be used as the selection devices, weighted 60% and 40% respectively. Although the weighting came about as a result of negotiations with the union, it was apparently not based on job analysis research. Candidates were required to be placed on the eligibility list in the rank order of their scores, even though the measurement properties of the tests used could not distinguish between candidates in such a finite manner. The City's charter requires promoting only from the highest scoring three candidates, called the "rule of three," even though there could be other candidates just as qualified but a few decimal points away in score. The examinations were administered in November and December of 2003, and the results of the exams are shown in Table 8-1.

Table 8-1. *Ricci* Exam Results

# in Group (Passing Rate %)				
Exam/Status	Total	White	Black	Hispanic
Lieutenant Exam (taking)	77	43	19	15
Lieutenant Exam (passing)	34	25 (58%)	6 (32%)	3 (20%)
Captain Exam (taking)	41	25	8	8
Captain Exam (passing)	22	16 (64%)	3 (38%)	3 (38%)

Under the rule of three, the top ten candidates were eligible for an immediate promotion to the eight open lieutenant positions. All ten were white. Subsequent vacancies would have allowed at least three black candidates to be considered for promotion to lieutenant. Seven captain positions were vacant at the time of the examination. Under the rule of three, nine candidates were eligible for an immediate promotion to captain (seven whites and two Hispanics).

After giving the tests and learning that there was substantial adverse impact on minority candidates (80% Rule violations[65] and various levels of statistical significance based on each exam and how the groups could be combined), the City discarded the test results. Their decision was based on the adverse impact finding as well as on limited information that the tests might not have survived a "possible" disparate impact challenge.

The City faced two choices, both involving possible lawsuits: (1) if the City kept the test results, there could be a lawsuit from minorities who would likely not have been appointed had the lists been adopted; or (2) if the City discarded the test results, there could be a lawsuit from whites who would have likely been appointed had the lists been adopted. A potential suit from whites would be a disparate treatment suit; the suit from minorities would be a disparate impact suit. The City elected to discard the exam results and face the possible disparate treatment type of lawsuit from whites.

The US Supreme Court ruled that the City's action was impermissible in this case: "Fear of litigation alone cannot justify the City's reliance on race to the detriment of individuals who passed the examinations and qualified for promotions. Discarding the test results was impermissible under Title VII." The Court further noted that a strong basis in evidence would be necessary for such drastic action to be allowed: "If, after it certifies the test results, the City faces a disparate-impact suit, then in light of today's holding the City can avoid disparate-impact liability based on the strong basis in evidence that, had it not certified the results, it would have been subject to disparate-treatment liability" (2009). The City did not provide the strong basis in evidence because they only presented unsupported arguments.

The Relevance of Ricci in the Public Sector

Because *Ricci* involved a promotional exam given to city firefighters (government employees), many might question the relevance of the case to private sector employers. However, both types of employers are subject to Title VII. Further, *Ricci* was decided on statutory grounds, not constitutional grounds. "We hold only that, under Title VII, before an employer can engage in intentional discrimination for the asserted purpose of avoiding or remedying an unintentional disparate impact, the employer must have a strong basis in evidence to believe it will be subject to disparate-impact liability if it fails to take the race-conscious, discriminatory action" (2009).

Because state and local government workers are public sector employers, their hiring, promotional, and contracting practices are covered by Title VII and are subject to the strict scrutiny theory of constitutional law. The Court used principles from constitutional cases for guidance: "Our cases discussing constitutional principles can provide helpful guidance in this statutory context" (2009).

The cornerstone case that pertains to the strict scrutiny and strong-basis-in-evidence standards in the public sector is *Richmond v. Croson* (1989). In *Croson*, the Supreme Court codified the strong-basis-in-evidence standard that originated three years earlier in *Wygant v. Jackson Board of Education* (1986). Both of these cases involved the strong-basis-in-evidence standard in ways that were relevant to the framework used in *Ricci*.

The *Croson* case involved a city program that set aside 30% of city construction funds for black-owned firms which was challenged under the Equal Protection Clause of the Fourteenth Amendment. This set-aside quota was judged as a "highly suspect tool" by the Supreme Court. The Court asserted that such affirmative action steps must be subject to "strict scrutiny" and are unconstitutional unless racial discrimination can be proven to be "widespread throughout a particular industry." The Court stated that "the purpose of strict scrutiny is to 'smoke out' illegitimate uses of race by assuring that the legislative body is pursuing a goal important enough to warrant use of a highly suspect tool. The [strict scrutiny] test also ensures that the [race-conscious] means chosen 'fit' this compelling goal so closely that there is little or no possibility that the motive for the classification was illegitimate racial prejudice or stereotype" (*Richmond v. Croson*, 1989).

Both public and private cases that have followed in the wake of the *Croson* decision have decided that affirmative action programs that use race-conscious remedies can pass the strict scrutiny test only if they are narrowly tailored toward eradicating the effects of past discrimination and preventing current/future discrimination. Narrowly tailoring the remedies means that they must take into account factors such as the necessity of the program and the plausibility of alternative remedies, the scope and duration of the remedy, the relationship of the numerical goals to minorities within the relevant labor market, and the likely effect on other gender or race/ethnic groups that are not part of the program.

Because private employers are not covered by the Fourteenth Amendment,[66] they may be held to a lesser standard than the strict-scrutiny standard. Nevertheless, the ruling in *Ricci* states that at least part of the Court's intention was to "provide guidance to employers and courts for situations when these two prohibitions [disparate-impact liability and disparate-treatment discrimination] could be in conflict absent a rule to reconcile them. In providing this guidance our decision must be consistent with the important purpose of Title VII—that the workplace be an environment free of discrimination, where race is not a barrier to opportunity" (2009). This admonition appears to speak to both public and private employers alike.

Clearly, the Court used concepts from prior constitutional cases and applied them in *Ricci*: "This suit does not call on us to consider whether the statutory constraints under Title VII must be parallel in all respects to those under the Constitution. That does not mean the constitutional authorities are irrelevant, however" (2009). The basic concept put forth by the Court in *Ricci* applies to public and private employers—before an employer can implement intentional discrimination on a protected group (race, color, religion, sex, national origin) for the purpose of avoiding a potential disparate impact liability, the employer must have a strong-basis-in-evidence standard that it will be subject to disparate impact liability if it fails to take the discriminatory action. The strong-basis-in-evidence standard is the common thread for both public and private employers and, since it is now a statutory standard, it must be applied in Title VII cases involving both public and private employers.

The Strong-Basis-in-Evidence Standard

In the *Ricci* case, the Supreme Court stated: "We hold only that under Title VII, before an employer can engage in intentional discrimination for the asserted purpose of avoiding or remedying an unintentional disparate impact, the employer must have a strong basis in evidence to believe it will be subject to disparate-impact liability if it fails to take the race-conscious, discriminatory action" (2009). The Court's analysis begins with the premise that the City's actions would violate the disparate-treatment provisions of Title VII unless there was some valid defense and reasons: "All the evidence demonstrates that the City chose not to certify the examination results because of the statistical disparity based on race—how minority candidates had performed when compared to white candidates.... Without some other justification, this express, race-based decision making violates Title VII's command that employers cannot take adverse employment actions because of an individual's race" (2009).

The Court clarified that the primary question being asked in the case was not whether the City's conduct was discriminatory, but whether it had a lawful justification for its race-based action: "We consider, therefore, whether the purpose to avoid disparate-impact liability excuses what otherwise would be prohibited disparate-treatment discrimination.... Our task is to provide guidance to employers and courts for situations when these two prohibitions could be in conflict absent a rule to reconcile them" (2009). The Court continues and clarifies that "fear of litigation alone cannot justify an employer's reliance on race to the detriment of individuals who passed the examinations and qualified for promotions" (2009) and concludes, "Even if respondents were motivated as a subjective matter by a desire to avoid committing disparate-impact discrimination, the record makes clear there is no support for the conclusion that respondents had an objective, strong basis in evidence to find the tests inadequate, with some consequent disparate-impact liability in violation of Title VII" (2009).

Regarding making changes to the tests after they had been given—up to and including discarding the results altogether—the Court ruled that a strong basis in evidence had to somehow be demonstrated on the record, which was not done by the City. Had the City conducted a Croson Study[67] (defined in detail later in this Chapter) for the at-issue jobs prior to the development of the selection processes, they may have been justified in implementing less extreme race-conscious remedies to identify substantially equally-qualified candidates for the lists with less adverse impact. For example, competency-based cutoff scores, setting weights less likely to adversely impact minorities that job experts would indicate could produce substantially equally qualified candidates, banding based upon the reliability of the tests to group substantially equally qualified candidates together, and so on.

In the public sector, rules are often set up by a merit system, negotiation with a union, tradition, or some other reason that can influence the type of selection procedures to be administered and their use. Here are some examples:

- Written tests might be specified as required.
- A 70% cutoff score might be required (rather than a competency-based cutoff score).
- Certain weights on tests might be required (rather than using job analysis data or having job experts establish the weights based upon their opinions of relevance to the at-issue jobs, perhaps combined with a competency-based cutoff).
- The rule of three might be required (rather than identifying those substantially, equally qualified candidates based upon the measurements of the tests).
- A rank-ordered list might be required (rather than grouping candidates who are substantially equally qualified together).

- A rigid banding based upon the same score might be required (rather than grouping substantially equally qualified candidates together).

Different practices, procedures, and tests measure different competencies—each with varying levels of psychometric precision—and they should be developed and used with respect to how they relate to the actual job requirements (more so than just tradition). The constraints outlined above are typically established so everyone going into the selection process knows the ground rules are not necessarily based on competency and finding the most qualified applicant. If a public entity has any of these constraints, the *Ricci* case presents a blueprint of what is needed to establish a strong basis in evidence before making race-conscious remedies.

A competency-based system can often reduce unnecessary adverse impact against groups protected by Title VII compared to a selection system with rigid constraints. Some tests can create less adverse impact than traditional paper-and-pencil tests and can provide very qualified candidates (Dean, Bobko, and Roth, 2008). These tests can measure important or critical parts of jobs not measurable with paper-and-pencil tests; however, the cost is usually higher, except when the number of candidates is small. Use of competency-based cutoff scores often provides more qualified candidates with less adverse impact than an arbitrary, fixed cutoff score, such as 70%. Using job analysis data or having job experts determine weights to be used by different parts of the selection process often gives much more flexibility to a public entity for obtaining very qualified candidates with less adverse impact than fixed weights not based on job analysis data or job-expert opinions. Using a banding process to group substantially equally qualified candidates based upon the reliability of the tests (how consistently the test measures what it is supposed to measure) used in the selection process can provide many more competent candidates with less adverse impact than a fixed rule of three.

Any changes made after test administration for the sole purpose of lowering adverse impact, such as altering cutoff scores, alternate use of qualified weights, and so on, may invite challenges. This is due to Title VII's prohibition against making race-based adjustment of test results. This is especially the case if they are outside of the substantially equally valid or substantially equally qualified doctrines or are not justified by the strong-basis-of-evidence standard; see the section below regarding applying the *Ricci* standard to common testing situations. *Ricci* holds that these changes should be made, based upon a strong basis in evidence, prior to the administration of the selection process (hence the need for a Croson Study prior to the implementation of a selection procedure).

Title VII does not prohibit an employer from considering, before administering a test or practice, how to design that test or practice in order to provide a fair opportunity for all individuals, regardless of their race. And when, during the test-design stage, an employer invites comments to ensure the test is fair, that process can provide a common ground for open discussions toward that end. We hold only that, under Title VII, before an employer can engage in intentional discrimination for the asserted purpose of avoiding or remedying an unintentional disparate impact, the employer must have a strong basis in evidence to believe it will be subject to disparate-impact liability if it fails to take the race-conscious, discriminatory action (2009).

The strong-basis-in-evidence standard does not have to be evidence that is provable in court:

> Applying the strong-basis-in-evidence standard to Title VII gives effect to both the disparate-treatment and disparate-impact provisions, allowing violations of one in the name of compliance with the other only in certain, narrow circumstances. The standard leaves ample room for employers' voluntary compliance efforts, which are essential to the statutory scheme and to Congress's efforts to eradicate workplace discrimination, …and the strong-basis-in-evidence standard appropriately constrains employers' discretion in making race-based decisions: It limits that discretion to cases in which there is a strong basis in evidence of disparate-impact liability, but it is not so restrictive that it allows employers to act only when there is a provable, actual violation. (2009)

Rule of Three in a Croson Study

Another practice that could be evaluated in a Croson Study is how top candidates are certified to an appointing authority for final appointment. The appointment certification procedure called the "rule of three" used by a public employer may adversely impact groups protected by Title VII. Any practice, procedure, or test that causes adverse impact on a group protected by Title VII in a hiring or promotion process is subject to a disparate-impact discrimination challenge. If an adverse impact analysis of the rank-ordered distribution of scores indicates adverse impact throughout the appointing-potential part of the list, the chances are very good that the rule of three will have adverse impact (as it is used to select three people at a time from the rank-ordered lists). If the Croson Study finds that the practice of the rule of three has adversely impacted a group or groups protected by Title VII, then the job-relatedness of the rule of three needs to be demonstrated. This will be hard to do when the psychometrics of a written test and oral interview will almost never be reliable enough to justify strict rank order in groups of just three candidates.

For example, in *Ricci*, using the known SDs of each test—typical reliability estimates of .90 for the written test (internal consistency) and .60 for the interview (inter-rater reliability)—and the actual correlations between these two tests ($r = .35$ and r = .40 for the lieutenant and captain positions, respectively), the composite reliability of the two combined measures can be estimated (r = .84 and r = .85 for the lieutenant and captain process, respectively). This value can be used with the SD of scores on each list to compute a SED that can be used to band applicants that are deemed substantially equally qualified. Multiplying the SED in this example by 1.96 provides a 95% confidence interval that applicants who are within a 9.12 point spread (for the lieutenant list) and 9.06 point spread (for the captain list) possess scores that are statistically indistinguishable. In other words, score differences within the broader extremes of this range can be considered the product of measurement error with these tests, rather than reliably different ability levels between the candidates.

With these ranges of substantially equally qualified candidates, there might be as few as two substantially equally qualified candidates for the appointing authority to consider, or as many as nine or more. It is unlikely that there will always be three. The reliability of the test is used to establish the measurement range of the test. The number of substantially equally qualified candidates will vary throughout the range of scores. But that's what a job-related selection procedure should be doing—reliably basing the grouping of candidates according to how their competency levels may differ.

Remember that the Supreme Court has stated that banding would not be an option after the fact if the sole reason for doing so is race-based. The decision to band needs to be made before test administration begins. "Had the City reviewed the exam results and then adopted banding to make the minority test scores appear higher, it would have violated Title VII's prohibition of adjusting test results on the basis of race." (2009). If a public entity performs a Croson Study, evaluates the rule of three as a part of that study, and finds adverse impact in the past, it is likely to happen again. Changing to a banding process after test administration will probably be too late, according to the Supreme Court, if the reason is race-based. Therefore, stating before test administration that banding will be used based upon the reliability of the tests involved in making the list is making adjustments on the basis of the test reliability, not race, and is a more prudent decision than waiting for a case to be filed after testing is done. Banding should be done based upon the measurement properties of the tests involved and not based upon an artificial number of three candidates at a time. The Croson Study can help act as the change agent to avoid disparate-impact discrimination liability because once adverse impact is shown on a current list with the rule of three, it is probably too late (see discussion on this specific topic later).

An inherent conflict exists between a civil service requirement that the selection process be job related and a requirement to use a rule of three. In the 1971 *Griggs v. Duke Power* (1971) case, the Supreme Court stated that the rule of three is a practice covered under Title VII: "Under the Act, practices, procedures, or tests neutral on their face, and even neutral in terms of intent, cannot be maintained if they operate to 'freeze' the status quo of prior discriminatory employment practices." The defendant City charter established a merit system. The merit system requires the use of job-related exams:

> When the City of New Haven undertook to fill vacant Lieutenant and Captain positions in its fire department (Department), the promotion and hiring process was governed by the city charter, in addition to federal and state law. The charter establishes a merit system. That system requires the City to fill vacancies in the classified civil service ranks with the most qualified individuals, as determined by job-related examinations. (2009).

The *Griggs* case, quoted above, tells us that "examinations" must be interpreted as "practices, procedures, or tests." The City's merit system states the requirement to use the rule of three:

> After each examination, the New Haven Civil Service Board (CSB) certifies a ranked list of applicants who passed the test. Under the charter's "rule of three," the relevant hiring authority must fill each vacancy by choosing one candidate from the top three scorers on the list (2009).

Perhaps the conflict between being required to use job-related practices as well as being required to use the rule of three was anticipated when the Supreme Court issued a clear warning to the public sector, in *Ricci*, that relying upon a state court's prohibition of banding may not be enough: "A state court's prohibition of banding, as a matter of municipal law under the charter, may not eliminate banding as a valid alternative under Title VII." (2009). Title VII states in part:

> Nothing in this subchapter shall be deemed to exempt or relieve any person from any liability, duty, penalty, or punishment provided by any present or future law of any State or political subdivision of a State, other than any such law which purports to require or permit the doing of any act which would be an unlawful employment practice under this subchapter.

A Croson Study can gather the data regarding adverse impact of the rule of three and crystallize the issue for public sector management to address before being required to by a court. With a Croson Study completed, more options are available to the public employer.

Applying the Ricci *Standard to Common Testing Situations*

What are the implications for employers of the Supreme Court's analysis of the test-related evidence that was available in the record? This was a unique case with unusual circumstances that are not typically encountered in EEO settings (tossing out a list solely on the basis that it had adverse impact against minorities and, as a result, having whites sue on the basis of disparate treatment). The classic Title VII burdens established under the US Supreme Court's unanimous ruling in *Griggs* and codified by the 1991 CRA remain intact. In the aftermath of *Ricci*, some recent lower-court cases clarified this point. For example, in the post-*Ricci* case of *United States v. City of New York* (2009), the court clarified that the *Ricci* case does not change the law as it relates to the burden-shifting requirements outlined in Title VII. While the major tenets of Title VII remain, *Ricci* does provide specific guidance to employers regarding making race-based decisions after an employment test has been given: let the results stand unless it can be proved (using the strong-basis-in-evidence standard) that the test is likely not valid or that other substantially equally valid (lower adverse impact) options were available but were overlooked.

Considering (1) the *Ricci* admonishment regarding changes after a selection process has been administered absent a strong basis in evidence that not acting will cause a disparate impact situation, (2) the "prohibition of discriminatory use of test scores" in Title VII's section 2000e-2(l), and (3) the alternate employment practices in Title VII's 2000e-2(k)(1)(A)(ii) (and related doctrine codified in the Uniform Guidelines, Sections 3B, 5G, 14B[5] and [6], and 14C[8] and [9] with respect to "alternate use with less adverse impact"), the following examples have been prepared to illustrate how employers can address real employment situations. Each example will be discussed in the context of the employers in situations with and without a strong basis in evidence, both before and after test administration.

Changing Weights

For the purposes of this discussion, the process of changing weights means changing from union-negotiated or arbitrary weights to a set of job-related weights based on job analysis data or ratings from a panel of job experts. Because developing test weights based upon job research results in weights that accurately reflect job requirements, such a process is actually likely to produce a more qualified applicant list than union-negotiated or arbitrary weights and may produce more or less adverse impact.

Changing weights before test administration with or without a strong basis in evidence

This practice is acceptable, even if adverse impact was a motivating factor behind starting the process to research and identify the actual job-related weights (based on both the "alternate employment practice" requirement of the 1991 CRA and the related "substantially equally valid" doctrine of the Uniform Guidelines). An example would be using the written test with a validated cutoff score as a pass/fail device only (especially if it only measures abilities needed at a baseline level, rather than differentiating abilities) and then weighting the test 100% (especially if it measured differentiating abilities).

Changing weights after test administration without a strong basis in evidence

This practice would not be defensible post-*Ricci*.

Changing weights after test administration with a strong basis in evidence

The Supreme Court ruled in *Ricci* that "changing the weighting formula, moreover, could well have violated Title VII's prohibition of altering test scores on the basis of race." (2009). Their key caveat to this statement was that "on this record, there is no basis to conclude that a 30% / 70% weighting was an equally valid alternative the City could have adopted" (2009). If, however, the City presented a set of weights (based on job analysis data or qualified job-expert opinions) that were substantially equally valid—or perhaps even more valid—than the original set used by the City, but reduced adverse impact, they might have been accepted. For example, if the City used job analysis data or job-expert opinions to determine that a 50% / 50% weighting scheme was substantially equally valid (or even more valid) than the 60% / 40% weights that were used, and the job related set reduced adverse impact, such a weighting scheme could have been adopted. However, merely suggesting alternative weights without also demonstrating that they were substantially equally valid to sufficiently address the alternate employment practice requirement of the 1991 CRA and the related substantially equally valid doctrine of the Uniform Guidelines would obviously not be acceptable, as they were rejected in the *Ricci* case.

Lowering Cutoffs

Because cutoffs split the entire applicant group into two groups—passing and failing—they should be set in a way that maximizes the differentiation between the qualified versus unqualified applicants. The most effective cutoff scores have the highest levels of DCR—a type of reliability that evaluates how consistently the test classifies "qualified" and "non-qualified," or those who pass the test versus those who fail (Biddle, 2006). Cutoffs that are set too high will eliminate too many applicants who are actually qualified. Cutoffs that are set too low have the opposite effect: they will select too many unqualified applicants. Cutoffs that are accurately set using a job-related process like the Angoff method are likely to have higher levels of DCR than arbitrary cutoffs. Even if a cutoff is set using a job-related method like the Angoff technique, the test used to measure applicant qualification levels along the continuum of scores will have a certain degree of score reliability with respect to measuring the same. As discussed earlier, accounting for this lack of perfect measurement can be done by reducing the cutoff score by one to three CSEMs. Also, discussed below is the possibility of lowering cutoffs without respect to the consideration of such measurement error.

Lowering cutoffs before test administration without a strong basis in evidence

Although this example implies lowering cutoffs in a way that is not based on the psychometric properties of the test (e.g., without considering the reliability or CSEM), it is likely defensible because it was done before the administration of the test. However, lowering cutoffs without respect to the psychometric properties of the test (or the ability continuum inherent within the score distribution) may possibly result in setting a standard that is below the qualification levels needed for the job. It is recommended to use the psychometric properties of the test and a job-related cutoff procedure.

Lowering cutoffs before test administration with a strong basis in evidence

If an employer determines a job-related cutoff before the test is given and desires to account for the measurement error of the test, he or she can defensibly lower the cutoff using CSEMs and determine the exact number (either one, two, or three) beforehand. Most CSEM methods require post-administration statistics for computation. However, the Lord-Keats method[68] can be used for estimating CSEMs before a test has been administered, although it is more advisable to simply state up front whether one, two, or three CSEMs will be deducted and then use the most accurate CSEM computations after test administration.

Lowering cutoffs after test administration with a strong basis in evidence

If an employer administers a test that is used with an arbitrary cutoff, and he or she subsequently determines that neither the test nor the cutoff score is sufficiently valid (establishing a strong basis in evidence), lowering the cutoff score to reduce or eliminate adverse impact may be permissible. In fact, the Court ruled in *Ricci* that having a strong basis in evidence may even justify a more severe action—retracting the test results altogether. Lowering the cutoff score with consideration of the psychometric properties of the test would be helpful to support this situation, as would knowing the test score level associated with the minimum levels needed for the job (e.g., a cutoff score set using the modified Angoff technique).

Lowering cutoffs after test administration without a strong basis in evidence

Provided that the employer lowers the cutoff based upon the psychometric limitations of the test, lowering the cutoff by one to three CSEMs may be permissible based on both the alternate employment practice requirement of the 1991 CRA and the related substantially equally valid doctrine of the Uniform Guidelines. It should be noted here that the race-norming prohibition of the 1991 CRA (§2000e-2[l]) expressly states that using different cutoff scores for different groups is prohibited; however, this should be differentiated from lowering a cutoff score, which is applied to all test takers in the distribution, within a range that is within the substantially equally valid confines. If the employer arbitrarily lowers the cutoff for race reasons only without a strong basis in evidence, this practice would not be supported post-*Ricci*.

Banding

As discussed previously, test score banding is widely practiced in the testing field and has been endorsed far more times than denied in litigation settings.[69] However, if banding is adopted after a test has been administered for the sole purpose of reducing adverse impact, the foundations laid down in *Ricci* apply as follows.

Banding before test administration with or without a strong basis in evidence

Before a test is administered, employers can predetermine to use banding, even though the span of the bands can only be determined after the test(s) have been administered (because the psychometric properties of the tests cannot be known until afterward).

Banding after test administration without a strong basis in evidence

This practice would not be permissible post-*Ricci*.

Banding after test administration with a strong basis in evidence

Provided that this process is based upon the psychometric properties of the test(s) involved, banding using one to three SED[70] may be permissible based on both the alternate employment practice requirement of the 1991 CRA and the related substantially equally valid doctrine of the Uniform Guidelines. Table 8-2 provides a summary of these recommendations.

Table 8-2 Strong-Basis-in-Evidence Requirement Applied to Testing Scenarios

Strong-Basis-in-Evidence Requirement (evidence of non-validity and/or no alternate employment practice)				
Practice	No Risk	Some Risk	Moderate Risk	High Risk
Changing weights	Before administration	After administration based upon correct math (e.g., using standard scores versus raw scores to weight tests)[1]	After administration based on updated/ corrected job analysis data or job experts panel opinions[2]	After administration, changing weights just to reduce adverse impact without job research[3]
Lowering cutoffs	Deciding to lower a job-related cutoff using one to three CSEMs before or after administration[4]	Deciding to lower an arbitrary cutoff before testing (not related to using one to three CSEMs)	Lowering an arbitrary cutoff score, after administration, just to reduce adverse impact	
Banding	Deciding to band before test administration	Banding based on arbitrary or weak statistical methods	Widening predetermined bands or deciding to band after administration, just to reduce adverse impact[5]	
Making adjustments after administration to avoid adverse impact	Considering future alternate employment practices with lower adverse impact, making changes, or validating for subsequent administrations	Removing test items based on qualified Differential Item Functioning (DIF) analyses[6]		Retracting or not certifying test results

[1]Changing from raw scores to standard scores will typically have an effect of changing the effective weights.

[2]Using accurate and reliable job analysis data and/or input from a panel of qualified job experts (such a change could result in higher or lower adverse impact).

[3] Note that the Court in *Ricci* ruled that changing the weights for the sole purpose of reducing adverse impact could likely violate the race-norming prohibition of the 1991 CRA (2009). Given the "could" caveat offered by the court, it is safe to say that weights that were not "substantially equally valid" would mostly likely constitute a violation; whereas, weights within a substantially equally valid range "may" cause a violation.

[4] This process is supported and based upon the psychometric characteristics of the test.

[5] In the *Ricci* decision, the Supreme Court addressed section 2000e-2(l), again dealing with the alternative employment practice of banding: "Here, banding was not a valid alternative for this reason: Had the City reviewed the exam results and then adopted banding to make the minority test scores appear higher, it would have violated Title VII's prohibition of adjusting test results on the basis of race." (2009).

[6] Removing test items based on DIF studies should be governed by the psychometric/validity properties of the item.

Endnotes

[1] For the purposes of this text, the terms *"disparate impact"* and *"adverse impact"* will be used interchangeably.

[2] Title VII Section 2000e-[k][1][A][ii][k] Burden of proof in disparate impact cases. (1) (A) An unlawful employment practice based on disparate impact is established under this subchapter only if (i) a complaining party demonstrates that a respondent uses a particular employment practice that causes a disparate impact on the basis of race, color, religion, sex, or national origin and the respondent fails to demonstrate that the challenged practice is job related for the position in question and consistent with business necessity; or (ii) the complaining party makes the demonstration described in subparagraph (C) with respect to an alternative employment practice and the respondent refuses to adopt such alternative employment practice. (B) (i) With respect to demonstrating that a particular employment practice causes a disparate impact as described in subparagraph (A)(i), the complaining party shall demonstrate that each particular challenged employment practice causes a disparate impact, except that if the complaining party can demonstrate to the court that the elements of a respondent's decision making process are not capable of separation for analysis, the decision making process may be analyzed as one employment practice. (ii) If the respondent demonstrates that a specific employment practice does not cause the disparate impact, the respondent shall not be required to demonstrate that such practice is required by business necessity. (C) The demonstration referred to by subparagraph (A)(ii) shall be in accordance with the law as it existed on June 4, 1989, with respect to the concept of "alternative employment practice."

[3] Readers interested in the historical and theoretical background of adverse impact are encouraged to read: Biddle, D.A. (2011). *Adverse impact and test validation: A practitioner's handbook* (3rd ed.). Scottsdale, AZ: Infinity Publishing.

[4] For an online tool to compute adverse impact, see http://www.disparateimpact.com.

[5] The Fisher Exact Test should not be used without this correction — see Biddle and Morris (2011).

[6] For example, see: *OFCCP v. TNT Crust* (US DOL, Case No. 2004-OFC-3); *Dixon v. Margolis* (765 F. Supp. 454, N.D. Ill., 1991); *Washington v. Electrical Joint Apprenticeship & Training Committee of Northern Indiana*, 845 F.2d 710, 713 (7th Cir.), cert. denied, 488 US 944, 109 S. Ct. 371, 102 L.Ed.2d 360 (1988); and *Stagi v. National Railroad Passenger Corporation*, No. 09-3512 (3d Cir. Aug. 16, 2010).

[7] For example, in Lanning v. Southeastern Pennsylvania Transportation Authority, (181 F.3d 478, 80 FEPC., BNA, 221, 76 EPD P 46,160 3rd Cir.(Pa.) Jun 29, 1999 (NO. 98-1644, 98-1755)), the court stated: "The District Court seems to have derived this standard from the Principles for the Validation and Use of Personnel Selection Procedures ("SIOP Principles").... To the extent that the SIOP Principles are inconsistent with the mission of *Griggs* and the business necessity standard adopted by the Act, they are not instructive" (FN20).

[8] While these guidelines are suitable for most tests that have either a single or a few highly-related KSAPCs being measured, sometimes wider guidelines should be adopted for multi-faceted tests that measure a wider range of competency areas (e.g., situational judgment, personality, behavior, bio-data tests).

[9] For example, see Bouman v. Block, 940 F2d 1211 (9th Cir. 1991); Hearn v. City of Jackson, Miss. 110 Fed. 242 (5th Cir. 2004); Isabel v. City of Memphis, F.Supp.2d 2003 (6th Cir. 2003); and Paige v. State of California 102 F.3d 1035, 1040(9th Cir. 1996).

[10] The steps outlined in this section are based on the requirements outlined by the Uniform Guidelines (1978), the Principles (2003), and the Standards (1999). The proposed model is not a one-size-fits-all process, but rather a generic template that could be employed in an ideal setting. While it is not *guaranteed* that, by following these steps, litigation will be avoided, implementing the practices outlined in this section will greatly increase the likelihood of success in the event of a challenge to a written testing process.

[11] The Uniform Guidelines do not require frequency ratings for content validity; however, obtaining frequency ratings provides useful information for addressing the 1990 Americans with Disabilities Act (ADA) and can also help when developing a test using content validity. Americans with Disabilities Act of 1990 (ADA), 42 USC §§ 12101-12213 2000). 1991 Civil Rights Act (42 USC §2000).

[12] Version 7, published in 2011.

[13] This rule-of-thumb time limit is only applicable for conventional multiple-choice tests. Where many calculations are needed for each test item (e.g., hydraulic items on a Fire Engineer test), obtain input from job experts to ensure an appropriate time limit.

[14] For an example, see Crocker and Algina, *Introduction to Classical and Modern Test Theory*, 1986.

[15] See Biddle (2011) or the Test Validation & Analysis Program (TVAP) for the recommended procedures for this step.

[16] In a meta-analysis conducted by Schmitt, Clause and Pulakos (1996), the mean standardized difference was -.09 for personality measures compared to -.83 for general cognitive ability. Various traits, however, will produce different subgroup gaps.

[17] This is an invaluable step because having two raters rate (at least a subset of) the employees will allow rater reliability to be evaluated, which will allow statistical corrections to be made to estimate the true (adjusted) levels of validity identified in the study.

[18] Because personality factors are complex, conducting a test-retest study is often the only way to ascertain the true reliability.

[19] Biddle Consulting Group, Inc., can be contacted via mail (193 Blue Ravine Road, Suite 270, Folsom, CA 95630) or phone (916-294-4250).

[20] For example, contact Biddle Consulting Group, Inc. for Biddle, D., Kuang, D., and Higgins, J. (2007). *Test use: Ranking, banding, cutoffs, and weighting*; and Biddle, D., and Feldt, L. 2011: *A new method for personnel score banding using the conditional.*

[21] Alternatively, Multiple-Response RASCH Modeling can be used for deriving a total score for each candidate (using the FACETS software program). When the RASCH method is used for analyzing rater data and scoring interviewees, raters should be "mixed" (randomly assigned to panels) and linked. FACETS can also be useful for evaluating rater bias. It is typically a good practice to complete the rater training process by holding one or two mock interviews and having the raters complete and pass a brief rater training test. The critical factor regarding rater training is that raters should share a similar frame of reference for what constitutes a strong, mediocre, and low scoring applicant on each of the scales.

[22] VO2 maximum refers to the highest rate of oxygen consumption attainable during maximal or exhaustive exercise.

[23] For example, see the US Equal Employment Opportunity Commission, Notice Number 915.002 at http://www.eeoc.gov/policy/docs/preemp.html (Date 10/10/95).

[24] Section 703 of the Civil Rights Act of 1964 (42 USC 2000e-2) (as amended by section 105) states: "It shall be an unlawful employment practice for a respondent, in connection with the selection or referral of applicants or candidates for employment or promotion, to adjust the scores, use different cutoff scores for, or otherwise alter the results of, employment related tests on the basis of race, color, religion, sex, or national origin."

[25] See, for example, *EEOC v. Dial Corp.*, 469 F.3d 735 (8th Cir. 2006). A major company lost a 3.4 million-dollar court case due to the fact that, during testing, job candidates were required to not only perform a work-related task at a faster pace than required to be performed on the job, but also without the short breaks between efforts that are allowed on the job.

[26] It should be noted that some situations might include job incumbents who are performing inadequately as an overall group. In this circumstance, deviations from the steps described herein may be made.

[27] For example, see: Weir, J. (2005). Quantifying test-retest reliability using the intraclass correlation coefficient and the SEM. *Journal of Strength Conditioning Research,* 19 (1), 231-240; Wang, C. and Chen, L. (2010). Grip strength in older adults: Test-retest reliability and cutoff for subjective weakness of using the hands in heavy tasks. *Archives of Physical Medicine for Rehabilitation, 91,* 1747-1751; Gross D. and Battie, M. (2002). Reliability of Safe Maximum Lifting Determinations of a Functional Capacity Evaluation. *Physical Therapy, 82* (4); Isernhagen S., Hart D. and Matheson L. (1990). Reliability of Independent Observer Judgments of Level of Lift Effort in a Kinesiophysical Functional Capacity Evaluation. *Work, 12,* 145-150; Reneman, M., Brouwer, S., Meinema, A. Dijkstra, P., Geertzen, J., and Groothoff, J. (2004). Test-retest reliability of the isernhagen work systems functional capacity evaluation in healthy adults. *Journal of Occupational Rehabilitation,* 14 (4), 295-305; Reneman, M., Dijkstra, P., Westmaas, M., and Göeken, L. (2002). Test-retest reliability of lifting and carrying in

a 2-day functional capacity evaluation. *Journal of Occupational Rehabilitation, 12* (4), 269-275; and Wang, C. and Chen, L. (2010). Grip strength in older adults: Test-retest reliability and cutoff for subjective weakness of using the hands in heavy tasks. *Archives of Physical Medicine for Rehabilitation, 91*, 1747-1751.

[28] This trend is typical in most studies conducted. For example, three other studies revealed negative correlations of r = - .65, r = - 60, and r = - .77 for department sizes of n = 61, n = 60, and n = 37, respectively. The authors acknowledge that some degree of this correlation is due to the auto-correlation that occurs with less time being available to correct with faster times, and more time with slower times (e.g., a 30-second adjustment on a 300-second score is 10%, whereas the same 30-second adjustment on a 600-second score is only 5%). However, each of the distributions studied revealed negative corrections almost always being made in the slower score ranges (where less time than the firefighter's time is recommended for the applicant).

[29] This study involved independent studies representing a total of 44 departments and 372 firefighters. The 5.56% was computed using a sample-size weighted applicant advantage across all four studies.

[30] For example, studies conducted by the authors revealed the PAT incumbent score data from 4 out of 5 fire departments (representing a combined sample size of 430 incumbents) to be significantly skewed, with skewness test results of 4.12, 3.24, 4.47, 1.86, and 2.77 (skewness test values are computed by dividing the skew value by the standard error of the skew, with values exceeding 2.0 indicate "significant" skew).

[31] Isserlis, L. (1918). On the value of a mean as calculated from a sample. *Journal of the Royal Statistical Society*, 81 (1), 75–81. (Equation 1)

[32] This will help to emphasize to the candidate the importance of safety on the job and will also help minimize potential grievances that might claim that the safety rules and/or safe working practices were not explained sufficiently.

[33] Test takers frequently do not accurately recall how well they performed during testing. For this reason, video- and/or audio-recording of test events will often enhance an employer's ability to successfully defend the elimination of an unqualified job candidate. As with all test-related documents, recordings should be retained in the event of challenge by job candidates, which can sometimes occur years after testing has taken place. In addition, recordings of job candidates should only be used for selection purposes.

[34] See the 1990 Americans with Disabilities Act, Section 1630.2(n).

[35] See Question #13 in the EEOC's *Enforcement guidance: Reasonable accommodation and undue hardship under the Americans with Disabilities Act document* at http://www.eeoc.gov/policy/docs/accommodation.html for more details.

[36] The study was conducted by the authors in 2011. The survey sample included 151 Fire Chiefs, 12 Assistant Fire Chiefs, 8 Battalion Chiefs, 6 Deputy Chiefs, 4 Deputy Fire Chiefs, 4 Division Chiefs (185 total). The average department size was 123, with an average of 109 active fire suppression personnel. The smallest department included had 9 full-time employees; the largest had 1,790.

[37] Fire & Police Selection, Inc. conducted this study in 2011, which involved firefighter incumbents from over forty fire departments for one PAT.

[38] The survey was limited to competency areas that can be measured in a testing process.

[39] If the test will be used to rank applicants, or a pass/fail cutoff that is above minimum competency levels will be used, the Best-Worker rating should also be used as a minimum criteria, with a minimum level set for selecting KSAPCs for the test (see Chapter 6).

[40] *"Discrete"* is used to refer to one specific construct, whereas *"divergent"* refers to the measurement of more than one construct.

[41] The developer may prefer to not allow job experts to review the test answer key because in some situations doing so can have an impact on their minimum passing ratings. Nonetheless, the answer key should always be verified by at least two people.

[42] Classical test analysis refers to the test analysis techniques that use conventional analysis concepts and methods. More modern test theories exist (e.g., Item Response Theory), but are not discussed in this text.

[43] For example, see *Edwards v. City of Houston*, 78 F.3d 983, 995 (5th Cir., 1996), and *Houston Chapter of the International Association of Black Professional Firefighters v. City of Houston*, No. H 86 3553, US Dist. Ct. S.D. Texas (May 3, 1991).

[44] For example, see: Mazor, K., Clauser, B.,and Hambleton, R. (1992), The effect of sample size on the functioning of the Mantel-Haenszel statistic. *Educational and Psychological Measurement*, *52*, 443-451; Narayanan, P. and Swaminathan, H. (1995), Performance of the mantel-haenszel and simultaneous item bias procedures for detecting differential item functioning. *Applied Psychological Measurement*, *18*, 315-328; and Swaminathan, H., and Rogers, H. (1990), Detecting differential item functioning using logistic regression procedures. *Journal of Educational Measurement*, *27*, 361-370.

[45] In any given criterion-related validity study, it is not likely that all items on the test will be statistically related to job performance (this is not the requirement for tests based on criterion-related validity, but rather that only the overall test is sufficiently correlated). However, if there is no *specific evidence* that the test item is related to job performance, while simultaneously there is *specific evidence* that the item could possibly be unfair to a certain group, it is justifiable to consider the item for removal (the other factors listed should also be considered).

[46] For example, see *Evans v. City of Evanston* (881 F.2d 382, 7th Cir., 1989).

[47] When tests are based on criterion-related validity studies, cutoffs can be calibrated and set based on empirical data and statistical projections that can also be very effective.

[48] For example, see *United States v. South Carolina* (434 US 1026, 1978), *Bouman v. Block* (940 F.2d 1211, C.A.9 Cal., 1991), and related consent decree.

[49] Various job expert sample sizes are suggested throughout this text. A minimum of four job experts is proposed in this section (rather than the minimum of seven used

elsewhere) because the exposure of confidential test information may be of high concern to the employer for completing this step.

[50] This five-year maximum recommendation is made only to possibly help reduce the upward rating bias described later in this chapter that sometimes occurs on rating panels. It is not an absolute requirement.

[51] For example, see Cizek, G., and Sternberg, R. (2001). *Setting performance standards: Theory and applications* (1st ed.).

[52] This standard deviation will serve to trim the average ratings that are in the upper or lower 5% of the distribution.

[53] Using a confidence interval of +/- 1.645 Standard Errors of Difference, within the unadjusted cutoff score.

[54] The standard error of the mean Angoff rating for the item can be computed by first computing the standard deviation of the Angoff ratings, then dividing this value by the square root of the number of ratings — e.g., = 10/sqrt(12) in Excel.

[55] The SED of the rater panel can be computed by first computing the SEM of the rater panel then multiplying this value by the square root of 2.

[56] For example, see Schmidt, F. (1991). 'Why all banding procedures in personnel selection are logically flawed', *Human Performance*, *4*, 265-278; and Zedeck, S., Outtz, J., Cascio, W., and Goldstein, I. (1991), 'Why do "testing experts" have such limited vision?' *Human Performance*, *4*, 297-308.

[57] One clear support for using banding as a means of reducing adverse impact can be found in Section 3B of the Uniform Guidelines, which states: "Where two or more selection procedures are available which serve the user's legitimate interest in efficient and trustworthy workmanship, and which are *substantially equally valid* for a given purpose, the user should use the procedure which has been demonstrated to have the lesser adverse impact." Banding is one way of evaluating an alternate use of a selection procedure (i.e., one band over another) that is substantially equally valid.

[58] See Section 14C4 of the Uniform Guidelines.

[59] In *Guardians v. CSC of New York* (630 F.2d 79). One of the court's reasons for scrutinizing the use of rank ordering on a test was because 8,928 candidates (two-thirds of the entire testing population) were bunched between scores of 94 and 97 on the written test.

[60] For example, see: Gatewood, R., and Field, H. (1994), *Human Resource Selection* (3rd ed.) Fort Worth, TX: The Dryden Press; Aiken, L. (1988). *Psychological Testing and Assessment* (2nd ed.). Boston, MA: Allyn & Bacon; and Weiner, E., and Stewart, B. (1984). *Assessing Individuals.* Boston, MA: Little, Brown.

[61] For selection procedures that are designed to directly mirror job duties (called "work-sample tests"), only test-duty (and not test-KSAPC) linkages are required for a content validity study (see Section 14C4 of the Guidelines). In this case, the Best-Worker ratings on the duties linked to the work-sample test should be the primary consideration for evaluating its use (i.e., ranking or pass/fail). For tests measuring KSAPCs (and not

claiming to be direct "work-sample tests"), the extent to which the selection procedure measures KSAPCs that are differentiating should be the primary consideration.

[62] For example, see Mosier, C. (1943). On the reliability of a weighted composite. *Psychometrika, 8,* 161−168.

[63] See Uniform Guidelines Questions & Answers #47, the Principles (2003), and Cascio, W. (1998), *Applied psychology in human resource management,* Upper Saddle River, NJ: Prentice-Hall, Inc. for more information on this approach.

[64] All references labeled as (2009) herein refer to *Ricci v. DeStefano*, 2009.

[65] An 80% violation occurs when the selection rate of the focal group is less than 80% of the reference group's selection rate. The 80% test is only sometimes used as a practical evaluation of possible adverse impact (statistical significance tests are the most definitive standard — see Biddle, 2006).

[66] US Constitution, Amendment 14: "All persons born or naturalized in the United States, and subject to the jurisdiction thereof, are citizens of the United States and of the State wherein they reside. No State shall make or enforce any law which shall abridge the privileges or immunities of citizens of the United States; nor shall any State deprive any person of life, liberty, or property, without due process of law; nor deny to any person within its jurisdiction the equal protection of the laws." The Equal Protection Clause limits only the powers of government bodies, and not the private parties on whom it provides equal protection.

[67] "Croson Studies" come from a 1989 Supreme Court decision that decided local governments could not establish preferences based upon race and gender unless there is proof of prior discrimination. Race is a suspect classification that is subject to strict judicial scrutiny. *Richmond v. Croson*, 488 US 469, (1989). A "Croson Study" is used to justify minority business participation that is narrowly tailored to remedy past discrimination.

[68] Most CSEM methods require post-administration statistics for computation. However, the Lord-Keats method can be used for estimating CSEMs before a test has been administered (see Lord, F. (1984). Standard errors of measurement at different ability levels. *Journal of Educational Measurement, 21,* 239-243).

[69] For example, see Aguinis, H. (2004). *Test-score banding in human resource selection: legal, technical, and societal issues.* Santa Barbara, CA: Praeger Publishers.

[70] For example, see Biddle, D. (2008). Overview of CSEM Methods. In Hurtz, G. (Chair), Integrating conditional standard errors of measurement into personnel selection practices. Symposium presented at the Annual Conference of the Society for Industrial and Organizational Psychology. San Francisco, CA, April 2008; and Biddle, D., Kuang, D., and Higgins, J. (2007). Test use: ranking, banding, cutoffs, and weighting. Paper presented at the Personnel Testing Council of Northern California, Sacramento.

References

AERA - American Educational Research Association, the American Psychological Association, and the National Council on Measurement in Education. (1999). *Standards: Standards for Educational and Psychological Testing.* Washington, DC: American Educational Research Association.

Anastasi, A., and Urbina, S. (1997). *Psychological Testing* (7th ed.). Upper Saddle River, NJ: Prentice Hall.

Anrig, G. (January, 1987). 'Golden rule: Second thoughts,' *APA Monitor.*

Barrick, M., and Mount, M. (1991). The big 5 personality dimensions and job performance: A meta-analysis. *Personnel Psychology,* 44, 1-26.

Biddle, D.A., and Bell-Pilchard, S.L. (2012). *Testing in the fire service industry: A handbook for developing balanced and defensible assessments.* Scottsdale, AZ: Infinity Publishing.

Biddle, D. (2011). *Adverse impact and test validation: A practitioner's handbook* (3rd ed.). Scottsdale, AZ: Infinity Publishing.

Biddle, D. (2006). *Adverse impact and test validation: A practitioner's guide to valid and defensible employment testing (*2nd ed.*).* Burlington, VT: Ashgate Publishing.

Biddle, D. (2005). *Adverse impact and test validation: A practitioner's guide to valid and defensible employment testing* (1st ed.). Burlington, VT: Ashgate Publishing Company.

Biddle, D., Kuang, D., and Higgins, J. (2007). *Test use: Ranking, banding, cutoffs, and weighting.* Sacramento, CA: Paper presented at the Personnel Testing Council of Northern California, Sacramento.

Biddle, D., and Morris, S. (2011). Using lancaster's mid-p correction to the fisher's exact test for adverse impact analyses. *Journal of Applied Psychology,* 96 (5), 956-965.

Bloom, B. (1956). *Taxonomy of educational objectives: The classification of educational goals: Handbook I, cognitive domain.* Toronto, NY: Longmans, Green.

Bobko, P., and Roth, P. (December, 2004). Personnel selection with top-score-referenced banding: On the inappropriateness of current procedures. *Journal of Selection and Assessment,* 12 (4), 291-298.

Cascio, W. (1998). *Applied psychology in human resource management*. Upper Saddle River, NJ: Prentice-Hall, Inc.

Contreras v. City of Los Angeles, 656 F.2d 1267 (9th Cir. 1981).

Dean, M., Bobko, P., and Roth, P. (2008). Ethnic and gender subgroup differences in assessment center ratings: A meta-analysis. *Journal of Applied Psychology*, 93, 685-691.

Dye, D., Reck, M., and McDaniel, M. (1993). The validity of job knowledge measures. *International Journal of Selection and Assessment*, 1 (3), 153-157.

Feldt, L., and Brennan, R. (1989). *Reliability. In R.L. Linn (Ed.), Educational Measurement* (3rd ed.). New York, NY: Macmillan.

Feldt, L., Steffen, M., and Gupta, N. (1985). A comparison of five methods for estimating the standard error of measurement at specific score levels. *Applied Psychological Measurement*, 9 (4), 351-361.

Gatewood, R., and Field, H. (1994). *Human resource selection*. Orlando, FL: The Dryden Press.

Golden Rule Life Insurance Company v. Mathias, 86 Ill.App.3d 323, 41 Ill. Dec. 888, 408 N.E.2d 310, (1980).

Griggs v. Duke Power, 401 US 424, (1971).

Haertel, E. (2006). Reliability. In R. L. Brennan. *Educational Measurement* (4th ed.). Westport, CT: Praeger Publishers.

Hearn v. City of Jackson, 340 F.Supp.2d 728, (2003). (United States District Court, S.D. Mississippi, Jackson Division, August 7, 2003).

Hunter, J., and Hunter, R. (1984). Validity and utility of alternative predictors of job performance. *Psychological Bulletin*, 96, 72-98.

Lanning v. Southeastern Pennsylvania Transportation Authority, 181 F.3d 478, 80 FEPC., BNA, 221, 76 EPD P 46, 160 3rd Cir. (Pa. June 29, 1999). (NO. 98-1644, 98-1755).

Lord, F. (1984). Standard errors of measurement at different ability levels. *Journal of Educational Measurement*, 21 (3), 239-243.

Narayanan, P., and Swaminathan, H. (1995). Performance of the mantel-haenszel and simultaneous item bias procedures for detecting differential item functioning. *Applied Psychological Measurement*, 18, 315-328.

NFPA- National Fire Protection Agency. (2000). *NFPA 1583: Standard on health-related fitness programs for fire fighters*. Quincy, Massachusetts: Author.

NIST - National Institute of Standards and Technology. (2005). *The economic consequences of firefighter injuries and their prevention. Final Report*. Arlington, VA: Author.

Officers for Justice v. Civil Service Commission. CA9, 1992, 979 F.2d 721, cert. denied, 61 U.S.L.W. 3667, 113 S. Ct. 1645, March 29th, (1993).

Peng, C., and Subkoviak, M. (1980). A note on Huynh's normal approximation procedure for estimating criterion-referenced reliability. *Journal of Educational Measurement*, 17 (4), 359-368.

Qualls-Payne, A. (1992). A comparison of score level estimates of the standard error of measurement. *Journal of Educational Measurement*, 29 (3), 213-225.

Ricci v. DeStefano, 129 S. Ct. 2658, 2671, 174 L. Ed. 2nd 490 (2009).

Richmond v. Croson, 488 US 469, 500 (1989).

Rudebusch v. Hughes, 313 F.3d 506 (9th Cir. 2002).

Sackett, P., Schmitt, N., Ellingson, J., and Kabin, M. (2001). High stakes testing in employment, credentialing , and higher education: Prospects in a post-affirmative action world. *American Psychologist*, 56, 302-318.

Siconolfi, S., Garber, C., Lasater, T., and Carleton, R. (1985). A simple, valid step test for estimating maximal oxygen uptake in epidemiologic studies. *American Journal of Epidemiology*, 382-390.

SIOP – Society for Industrial Organizational Psychology. (1987, 2003). *Principles for the validation and use of personnel selection procedures* (3rd and 4th Editions). College Park, MD: SIOP: Author.

Subkoviak, M. (1988). A practitioner's guide to computation and interpretation of reliability indices for mastery tests. *Journal of Educational Measurement*, 25 (1), 47-55.

Tabachnick, B., and Fidell, L. (1996). *Using multivariate statistics* (3rd ed.). New York, NY: Harper Collins.

Tsutakawa, R., and Johnson, J. (1990). The effect of uncertainty of item parameter estimation on ability estimates. *Psychometrika*, 55, 371-390.

EEOC - Equal Employment Opportunity Commission, Civil Service Commission, Department of Labor, and Department of Justice, Adoption of Four Agencies of Uniform Guidelines on Employee Selection Procedures, 43 Federal Register,

38,290-38,315 (August 25, 1978). *Uniform Guidelines.* Equal Employment Opportunity Commission, Office of Personnel Management, Department of Treasury, Adoption of Questions and Answers to Clarify and Provide a Common Interpretation of the Uniform Guidelines on Employee Selection Procedures, 44 Federal Register 11,996-12,009 (1979).

US Department of Labor: Employment and Administration Training (2000). *Testing and assessment: An employer's guide to good practices.* Washington, D.C.: Department of Labor Employment and Training Administration.

US v. South Carolina, 434 US 1026, (1978).

Wilcox, R., and Keselman, H. (2003). Modern robust data analysis methods: Measures of central tendency. *Psychological Methods*, 8 (3), 254–274.

Wilcox, R., and Keselman, H. (2003). Repeated measures one-way anova based on a modified one-step m estimator. *British Journal of Mathematical and Statistical Psychology,* 56, 15-26.

Wygant v. Jackson Board of Education, 476 US 267 (1986).

Index

A

administering tests

    personality tests 29

adverse impact.. 4

    the trigger for title VII litigation........... 4

age and gender norming 67

Americans with Disability Act (ADA) and

    Physical Ability Testing (PAT)............ 59

applying *Ricci* standards

    common testing situations 126

B

banding.......................... 102, 103, 129, 130

behavioral questions................................. 35

benefits of the validation process 15

Biddle Consulting Group, Inc. (BCG)..... 24

Boston Chapter, NAACP Inc. v. Beecher 105

Brunet v. City of Columbus.................... 105

building a balanced hiring program......... 69

building a balanced testing program

    challenges and recommendations 71

C

Chi-Square computation........................... 6

Civil Rights Act (CRA)

    1991 2

    Section 703 [k][1][A][i]...................... 15

civil rights enforcement agencies

    US Equal Employment Opportunity

        Commission (EEOC) and the Office

        of Federal Contract Compliance

        Programs (OFCCP)......................... 1

Clady v. County of Los Angeles..............105

classical test analysis.............................. 83

    item-level analyses.............................. 83

    test-level analyses.............................. 89

competency-based questions................... 36

    example 36

Conditional Standard Error of

    Measurement (CSEM)....25, 91, 93, 95,

    98, 99, 102, 104, 128, 130

confidence intervals................................ 91

connecting a test to a job........................ 13

construct validity.................................9, 11

content validity..............................9, 11, 13

    conducting job analysis research........ 13

    proposed solutions for personal

        characteristics of entry-level

        Firefighters 73

    proposed solutions for testing physical

        abilities of entry-level firefighters . 73

    testing cognitive/academic competencies

        of entry-level firefighters............... 72

Contreras v. City of Los Angeles

    five (5) out of seven (7) rule.............. 82

correlation strength 30

criterion-related validity.................9, 11, 25

    concurrent model................................ 14

    how to find criterion-related validity.. 14

    predictive model................................. 14

    proposed solutions for personal

        characteristics of entry-level

        firefighters 73

proposed solutions for testing physical abilities of entry-level firefighters . 73

sample size 14

steps to follow to conduct a predictive criterion-related validity study 14

testing cognitive/academic competencies of entry-level firefighters 72

Cronbach's Alpha 90

croson study

Rule of Three.................................. 123

using croson studies to develop defensible diversity initiaves........ 117

D

Decision Consistency Reliability (DCR).....

.... 90, 93, 127

limited, good, and excellent values..... 94

descriptive analyses................................. 89

descriptive test analyses 89

mean and standard deviation 89

developing a clear test plan 13

developing test content.......................... 23

developing valid cutoff scores................. 95

developing, validating, and analyzing written tests.. 75

Differential Item Functioning (DIF)....... 83, 84, 86, 130

considerations to make before removing items.. 87

evaluating DIF with the Mantel-Haenszel Method 86

example 88

sample size requirements.................... 86

disparate impact.............................. 2, 118

disparate treatment 3, 118

E

Educational Testing Service 85

EEOC 1, 6, 9, 11, 43, 59, 60

Equal Employment Opportunity Act of 1972.. 2

Estimated True Score (ETS)................... 98

evaluating the relevance of *Ricci* in both public and private sectors.................. 119

F

face validity.. 15

factor analysis 29

fairness study 31

fire-safety chief survey........................... 69

focal group 5

G

Griggs v. Duke Power 1, 2, 3, 124

Rule of Three....................................124

H

Hearn v. City of Jackson 88

I

internal consistency

reliability 88

interviews

administering and scoring an interview 40

developing, validating, and analyzing structured interviews 33

methods for improving the interview process 33

rating errors 40

situational questions 35

144

structured interview
content/methodology 34
types of questions to include in
structured interviews...................... 34
item-level analyses 83
items
item difficulty 84
rating questions for items 81
reverse scoring items 30
situational items................................. 35
types of items..................................... 79
validation criteria for items................. 82

J

job analysis........................... 23, 75, 96, 108
steps to conduct a job analysis............ 17
job duties
differentiating Best-Worker ratings 19
frequency 18
importance 18
KSAPC-linkage scale 20
mastery level...................................... 19
needed upon hire................................. 19
job experts 14, 21
minimum thresholds of endorsement
necessary from job experts 82
preparing the job experts for developing
situational questions...................... 38
job-knowledge tests
high reliability levels 21
job performance rating surveys 28

K

kappa coefficients........................ 90, 93, 94
levels of effectiveness......................... 94

Knowledge, Skills, Abilities, and Personal
Characteristics (KSAPCs)
complexity.. 77
KSAPCs 13
necessary number of items 78
Kuder-Richardson 20 (KR-20)................ 90
Kuder-Richardson 21 (KR-21)................ 91

L

legal requirements for validation
benefits of validation.......................... 12
techniques and requirements for testing
.... 12
when tests exhibit adverse impact 12

M

mastery-based tests 93
Decision Consistency Reliability (DCR)
.... 93
Modified Angoff 24, 96, 101
setting cutoffs that are higher than the
established minimum level 101
steps for developing and using the
Modified Angoff cutoff................. 96

O

Office of Federal Contract Compliance
Programs (OFCCP) 1, 11

P

Pearson Correlation................................. 15
how to perform the Pearson Correlation
in Microsoft Excel 15
personality tests
developing test items to target traits... 27

how to develop a validated personality test.. 26

lie scales 28

steps for developing a personality test using criterion-related validity 25

strategically building a personality test 29

the Big 5 27

Physical Ability Tests (PATs)

job analysis 44

maintenance standards within fire safety 62

pass/fail criteria 62

scoring PATs 58, 61

static strength tests 43

steps for developing PATs using criterion-related validity 46

steps to take with incumbents who fail annual maintenance standards 66

point biserials 83

using a Pearson Correlation matrix..... 83

post-administration analyses 25

problem-solving processes 22

process-by-content matrix 22

professional and government validation standards... 11

professional standards for validation......... 9

psychometric analyses 89, 90

Cronbach's Alpha.............................. 90

for mastery-based tests 93

how to obtain standard deviations 91

Kuder-Richardson 20 (KR-20) 90

Kuder-Richardson 21 (KR-21) 91

test reliability 90

true scores 91

p-value 5

Q

qualitative reasons why the item could be flagged as DIF 87

R

ranking 95, 102, 103

rating errors

central tendency................................. 41

halo.. 41

leniency 41

severity 41

similar-to-me 41

reference group 5

reliability

internal reliability standard................. 31

Ricci v. DeStefano 3, 117, 118, 119

Richmond v. Croson 119

S

scoring tests

compensatory tests 76

multiple-hurdle tests........................... 76

power tests.. 76

speeded tests....................................... 76

selection plan 75, 80, 81, 82

develop a selection plan 20

selection tools.. 17

SIOP Principles 10

situational questions

steps for developing situational questions.. 37

typical validity coefficients 35

split-half/hold-out

steps to conduct a

"calibration/validation" study 30

validation 29

Stagi v. National Railroad Passenger Corporation 6

Standard Error of Difference (SED) 50, 102, 124

Standard Error of Measurement (SEM) ......

.... 49, 50, 90, 91, 92, 99

confidence intervals 91

formula 49

Standard Error of the Mean 54

Formula 54

Standard Error of the Mean (SE Mean) ... 49

formula 54

standard scoring 41

standardizing scores 109

Standards and Principles

five sources for generating validity 10

Standards for Educational and

Psychological Testing 10

statistical measures

z values (or scores) 86

statistical significance 5

correlation coefficient 15

steps for developing a Physical Ability Test

using content validity 44

steps for developing content-valid hiring

assessments 17

strick-rank ordering

selection procedures 102

strong-basis-in-evidence standard 123

T

test plan 21, 75

choosing the number of items 77

choosing the type of items 78

developing the content 80

general components 76

test reliability 90, 92

test time limits 25

Test Validation & Analysis Program

TVAP 24

test-level analyses 83

the Fisher's Exact Test with Lancaster's

mid-P Correction 6

Title VII 2, 3, 4, 117, 118, 119, 120, 121, 122, 123, 124, 125, 126, 127, 130

U

Uniform Guidelines (UG) 1, 2, 5, 18, 19

1978 9

benefits of following the UG. 11

Section 4D 6

US v. City of New York 126

US v. South Carolina 99

63% rule 82

using selection procedures

cutoffs, banding, and ranking 94

V

validation report

benefits of completing a validation

report 32

validity 2, 3, 9, 10, 11

construct 9

content 9, 17

criterion-related 9

evidence 10

Vulcan Society v. City of New York

2009 3

W

Ward's Cove Packing Co. v. Atonio 2

Watson, 487 US at 994-95 6

weighting tests

    polytomous weighting 78

written tests

    delivery method 76

    determining KSAPCs to measure on the

        test 75

    developing a test plan 75

    reading level 76

    scoring and analyzing 83

    validation 81

Wygant v. Jackson Board of Education ....

.... 117, 119

Z

Z scores 41

Zamlen v. City of Cleveland 105

8

80% test 5

CPSIA information can be obtained at www.ICGtesting.com
Printed in the USA
LVOW05s1132050813

346185LV00001B/5/P